PEACEHA̵ ̵ ̵ ̵ ̵ ̵ ̵ ̵ ̵
TELSCOMBE

THROUGH TIME

Stanley Bernard

AMBERLEY PUBLISHING

First published 2009

Amberley Publishing
Cirencester Road, Chalford,
Stroud, Gloucestershire, GL6 8PE

www.amberley-books.com

British Library Cataloguing in Publication Data.
A catalogue record for this book is available from the British Library.

ISBN 978 1 84868 199 6

Typesetting and Origination by Amberley Publishing.
Printed in Great Britain.

Introduction

Peacehaven is relatively new – it was founded out of one man's vision of how to use an open space. It was developed out of the old parishes of Telscombe and Piddinghoe, both of which have changed because of the development of Telscombe Cliffs and Peacehaven. Telscombe can be traced back to around 966 or thereabouts when it was mentioned in an Anglo-Saxon charter, although it did not appear by name in the Domesday Book of 1086. Piddinghoe is thought to be equally old, with its church built on the site of a pagan place of worship. After the Norman Conquest both Telscombe and Piddinghoe were held by William de Warenne, a relative of William the Conqueror.

It was not until the time of Henry VIII's reformation that we can really trace the history of the older villages. When the priory of Lewes was dissolved Thomas Cromwell, Henry VIII's vicar general decided to keep the land owned by the priory for himself, this included Telscombe and some of Piddinghoe. He did not hold it for long as in 1540 he was executed, the same year that Henry divorced Anne of Cleves. In her divorce settlement she ended up with most of Cromwell's lands, which she held until her death in 1557.

Elizabeth I inherited Anne's land holdings and in an effort to raise money sold them off, some like Telscombe were bought by family members. Sir Thomas Sackville rose to the title of Lord Buckhurst and later as Earl of Dorset is recorded as Lord of the Manors of Telscombe and Piddinghoe. His family were to either own the land or be connected to the area for many centuries.

Telscombe was fortunate that during the centuries it attracted a number of charitable individuals. The first was Henry Smith who around 1658 bought, it is recorded, 217 acres of Telscombe. In that year under his will the Henry Smith Charity ran the estate for the benefit of the poor of six other villages, so Telscombe's inhabitants appear not too poor. Next on the death of Rev. Josiah Povey in 1727, a school was set up in his stables, to teach the children of the village to read, write and sew. The school was to change over time but only ceased in the twentieth century. The charity lives on, being administered by Telscombe Town Council for the benefit of children of Telscombe Cliffs County Primary School.

Ambrose Gorham is remembered both for his horse Shannon Lass winning the Grand National in 1902, as well as bringing electricity and water to the village of Telscombe in July 1909. It is because of his love of the village that it never changed and remains almost as it was when he purchased the Stud Farm, after his horse's triumph. Both Ambrose Gorham and Ernest Thornton-Smith, who gave the manor house to the National Trust, paid for repairs to the church of St. Lawrence in the village.

So how did Peacehaven and Telscombe Cliffs come about? It all started in 1898 when The Cavendish Land Company who had recently purchased about 222 acres of Telscombe, decided to develop the area. They held an auction in which they for the first time called the coastal strip of the parish Telscombe Cliffs. It was advertised as 'the newest and brightest seaside resort near London'. Although many plots were sold only the hotel, restaurant and estate office, all one building, was erected. This was eventually to become the Cliffs Club before its rebuild as Telscombe Civic Centre.

At the Newhaven end of the coast road, and still in Piddinghoe was the Friars Bay Estate that the executors of the Earl of Sheffield sold around 1909. Mr A. Harper Bond was the purchaser; he tried selling it as six smaller plots for small holdings as promoted by the then government. Mr Harrison of Leeds was purchased a plot from him to set up the Friars Bay Small Holders Colony, later to be known as Cliffs Park Estate.

In 1912 the Earl of Chichester sold the outlying portions of Stanmer Estates, which included Piddinghoe. Cavendish Land at that sale bought the 859 acres Hoddern Farm part of the estate. At some point in 1915 Charles William Neville, born in County Durham and educated in Canada, saw the estate. He had learned how to deal in real estate in Canada and Australia, so when he came to Piddinghoe he saw the opportunity. Setting up an office in London he bought much of Hoddern Farm. And through a major newspaper competition to name his new town Peacehaven was born. Two prize winners in 1916 named the town as New Anzac-on-Sea. A year later during the protracted court case against the *Daily Express*, Charles Neville changed the name to Peacehaven. Building could not start until 1920 when the Sussex War Agricultural Committee handed the land back to the South Coast Land and Resort Co. Ltd.

Today, what we see is a town started by one man and through compulsory purchase has been redesigned by various district plans.

Stanley Bernard

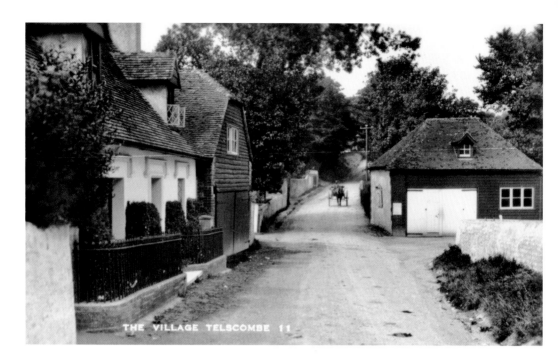

Telscombe village, a view looking past the school house up the road that rises through the downs before dropping down to the C7 road which skirts Piddinghoe. The transport in possibly the 1920s was still the horse and cart for working on the nearby farms. This old card was posted in 1936. Today, though a quiet road, a motor car is always present.

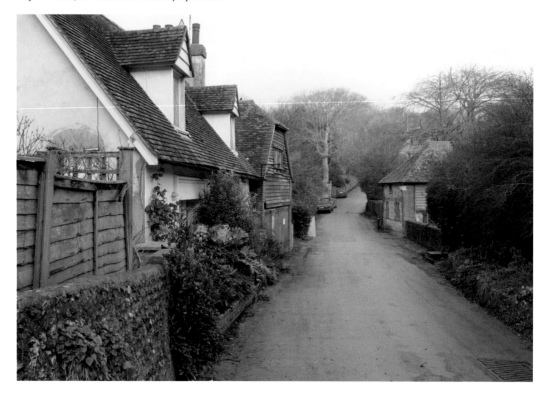

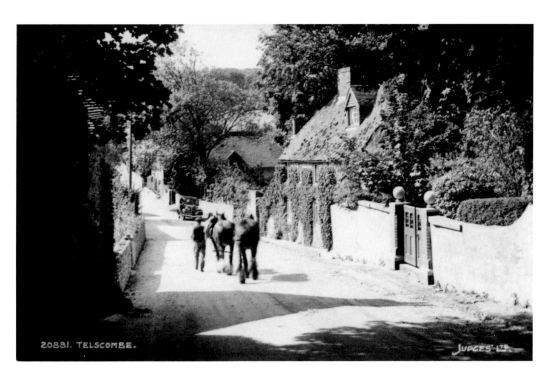

Telscombe village, a view looking back through the village, showing horses being led back to a farm. They appear to be farm horses on this card. Telscombe was also the home to the Stud Farm that bred and trained race horses.

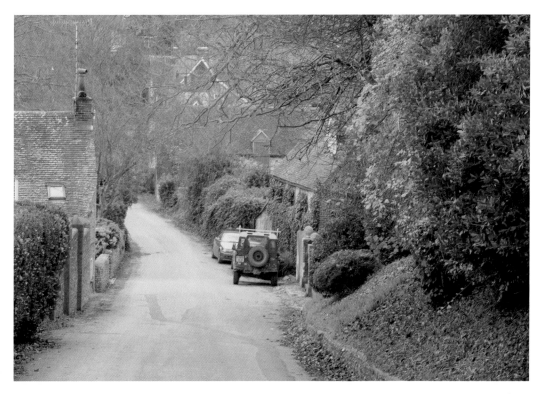

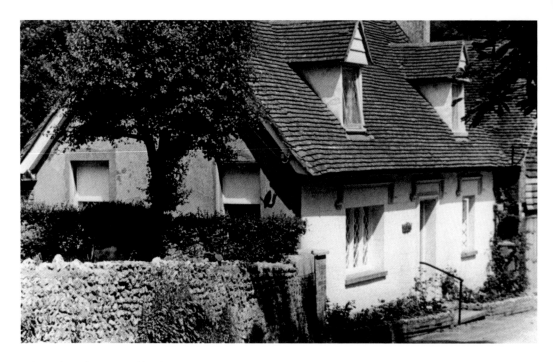

Telscombe village, the Old School House, now a private residence. It was possibly the site of the stable that the Rev. Josiah Povey left in his will of 1727 as a school he set up for the children of the village to read, write and sew.

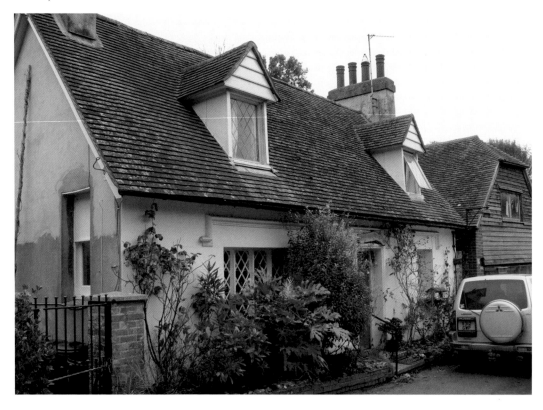

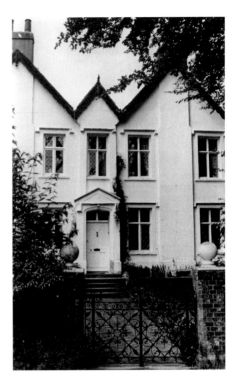

Telscombe village, the old rectory was the home of the rector of St. Lawrence. Although not officially joined to the parish of Piddinghoe until 1877, when George Hutchins was the rector of Telscombe and Vicar of Piddinghoe. There was an earlier record that after his appointment as rector of Telscombe, James Mills father paid for him become vicar of Piddinghoe in 1727.

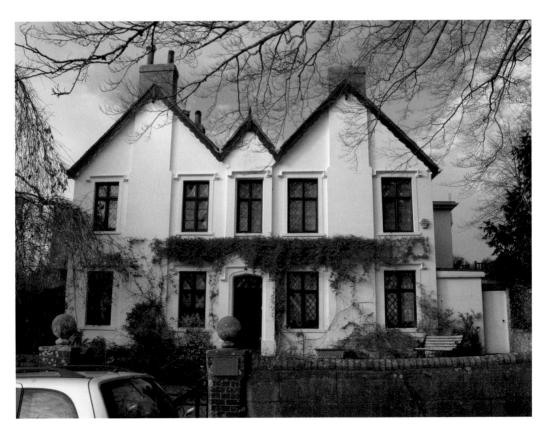

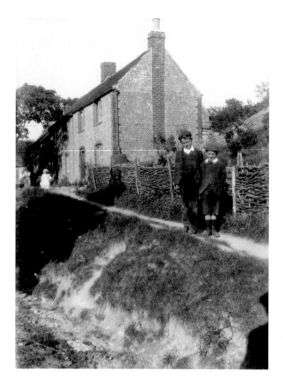

Telscombe village, taken from a photograph album of the Lord of the Manor, Ambrose Gorham in 1904, the Charity Cottages now Bank Cottages home of Telscombe Youth Hostel.

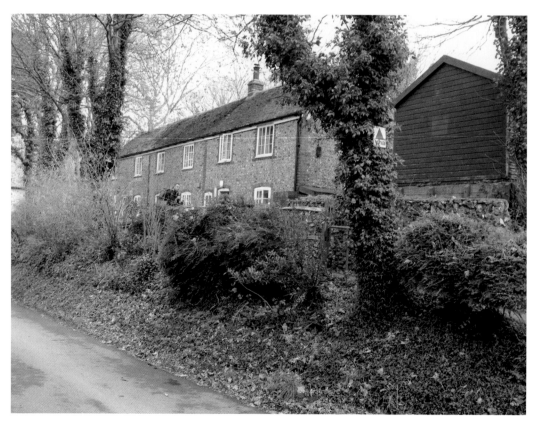

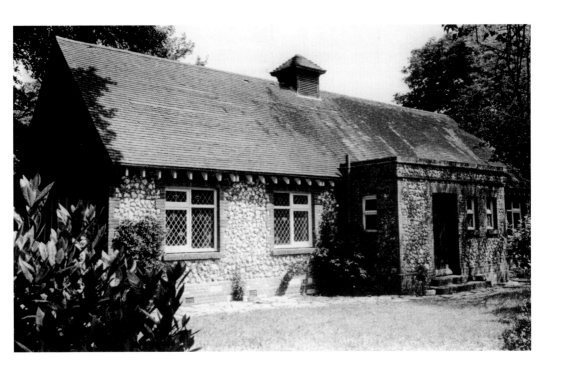

Telscombe Club built by Ambrose Gorham in 1924. It was built for the benefit of the villagers of Telscombe and until it was stolen in 1951, the home of the winners cup of 1902, when his horse Shannon Lass won the Grand National.

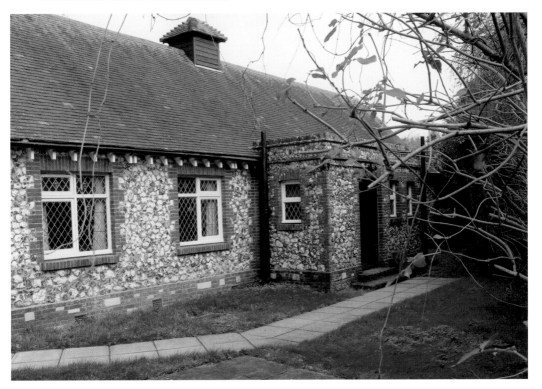

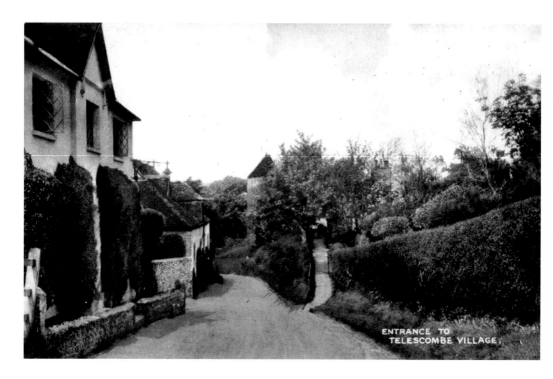

Telscombe village, coming into the village with the path leading to Bank Cottages barely visible to the right.

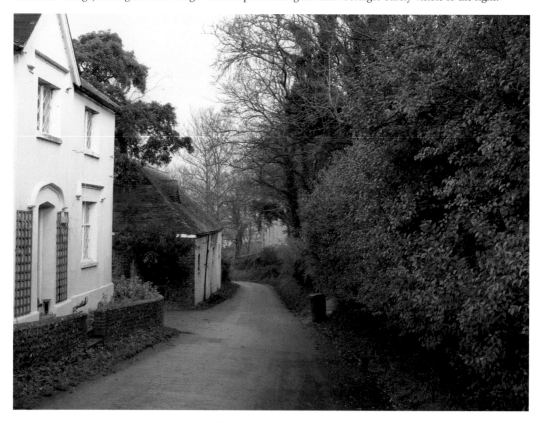

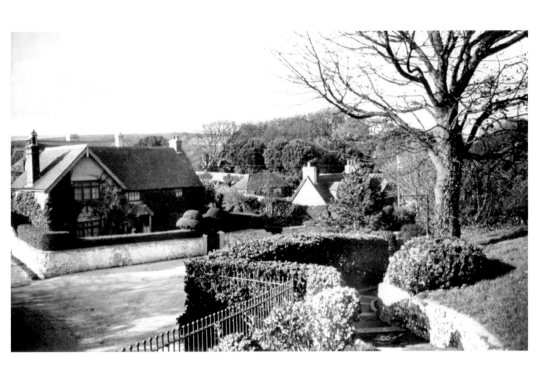

Telscombe village a view from the church down the path to the village street. The Old School House is just visible to right of the path.

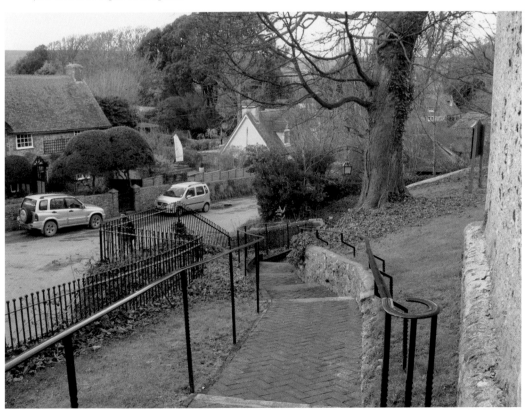

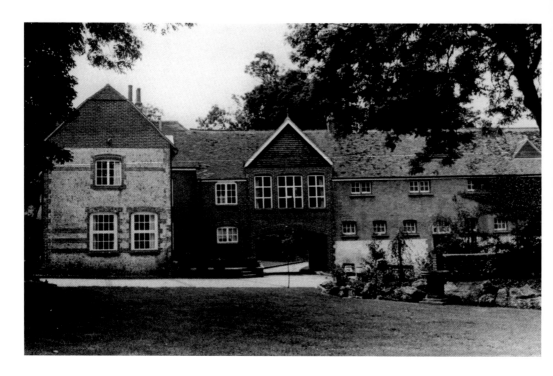

Telscombe village the Stud farm once owned by Mr Ambrose Gorham. At the time of Smith Charity it was known as Charity Farm. The charity had owned it from 1658 until 1920. Ambrose Gorham had, until that time, been the tenant.

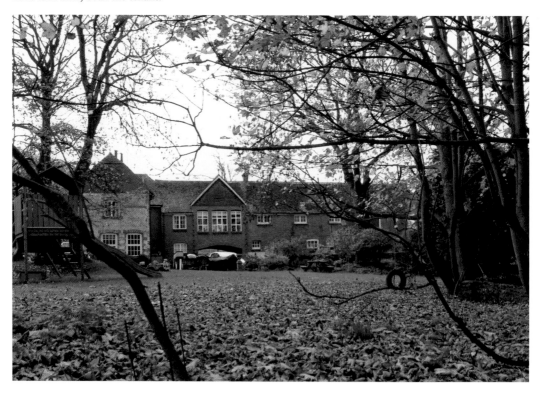

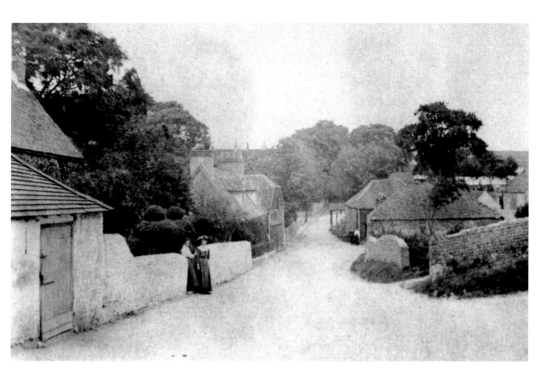

Telscombe village north of the school house looking down the road photographed in 1905 by Mary Pool, daughter of the then rector. Just visible is the village well once situated roughly outside the club house. Ambrose Gorham brought water to the village in 1909.

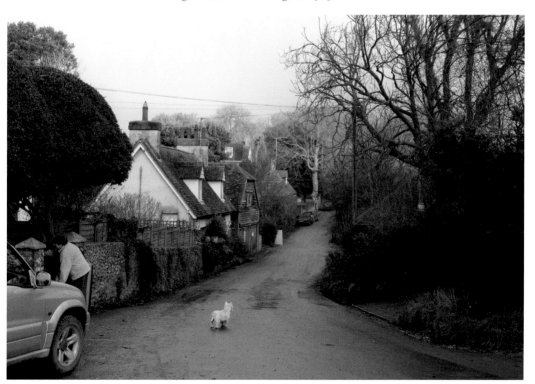

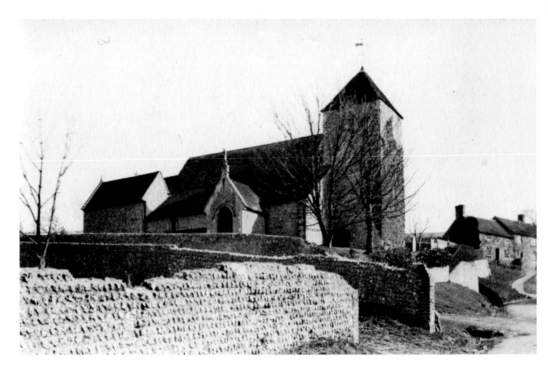

Telscombe village, the church. A rare 1906 photograph taken by the rector's daughter Mary Pool in winter of that year. The field to the left of the church has now been sold off and is now a private residence, know as Duck Barn.

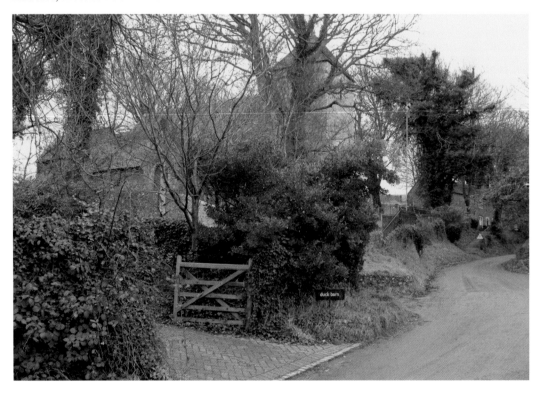

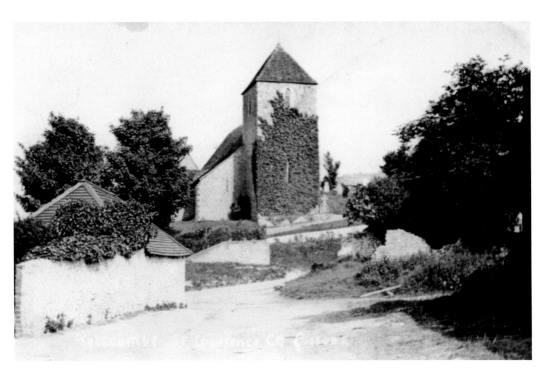

Telscombe village, view of the front of the church tower, a Mary Pool photograph of 1905 shows the wall in bad state of repair.

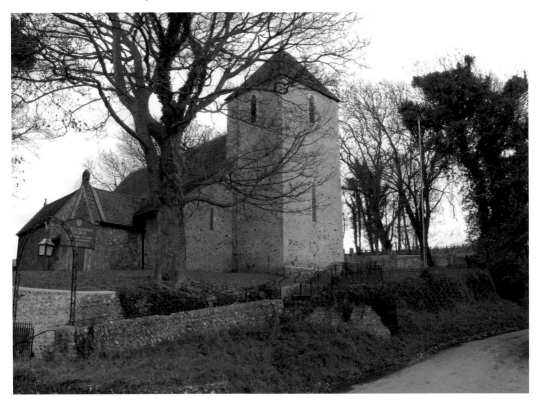

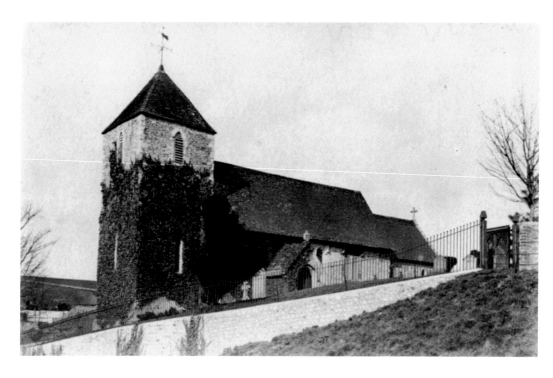

Telscombe village from the graveyard south side again, a Mary Pool photograph.

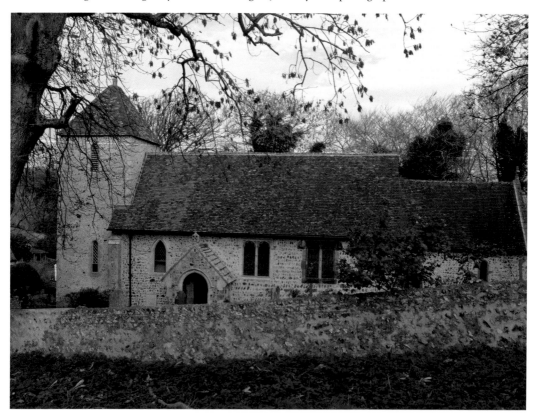

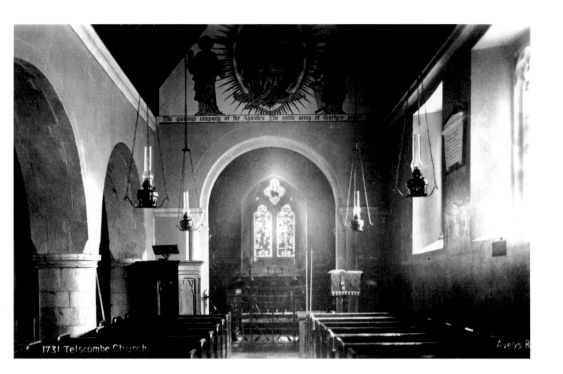

1731 Telscombe Church

Telscombe Church; being the rector's daughter, Mary Pool was able to take this photo from inside the church. Frederick Pool was rector from 1901 until 1910, and during that time his daughter took a number of pictures, only a few were saved. Parts of the church date back to Norman times.

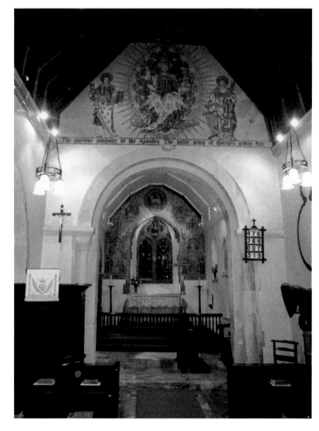

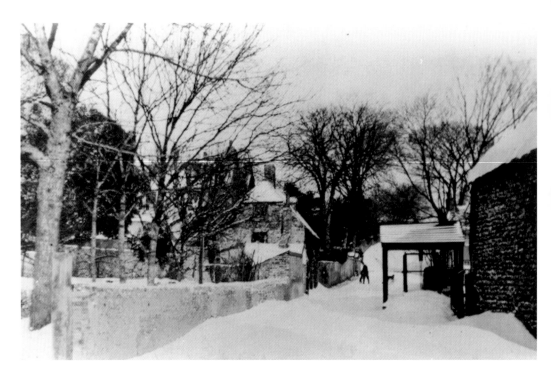

Telscombe village, this picturesque winter view of the village shows the village well, so it must date prior to 1909 when mains water was laid on by Ambrose Gorham. Now on the right is the entrance to Telscombe Club, which he also built.

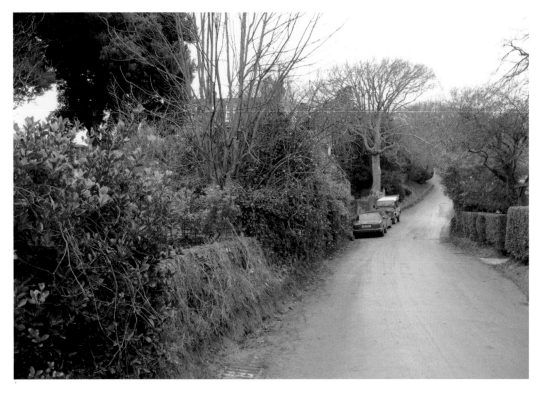

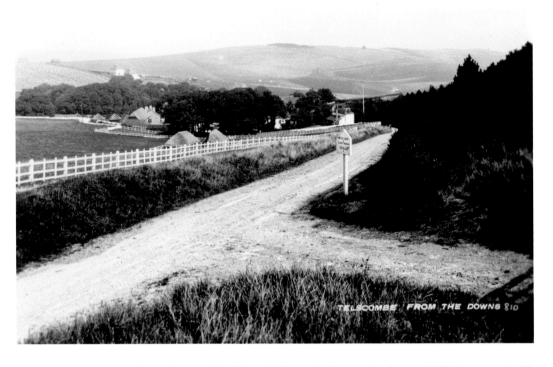

As you come over the Tye down to the village of Telscombe the sign asks for careful driving – now it aids walkers as it is designated a bridleway. The Tye came into being following the 1810 Act of Enclosure.

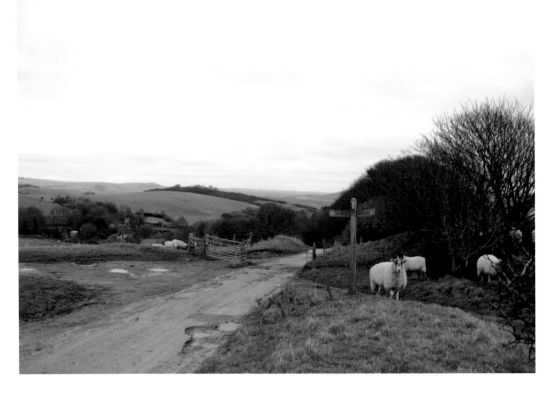

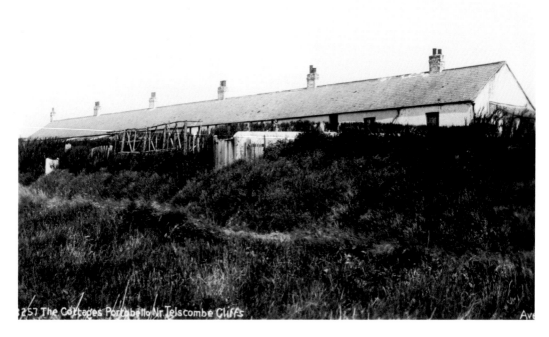

Telscombe town; the oldest buildings are the coastguard cottages which were on the old toll road. Possibly dating back to 1841 when Charles Beard leased the land to H M Customs at an annual rental of £81 per year.

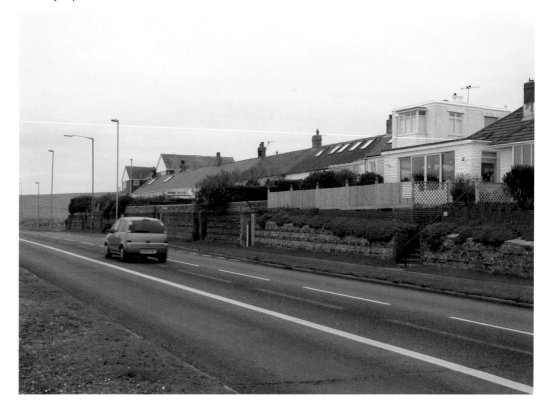

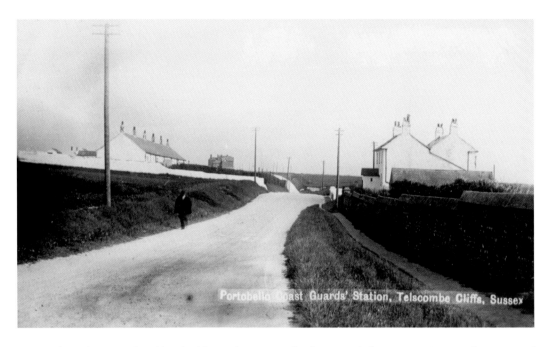

Portobello Coast Guards' Station, Telscombe Cliffs, Sussex

Telscombe town the oldest buildings showing in the foreground the Brewers Arms and Coastguard Cottages to the rear in the far distance is the first building erected by Cavendish Land Co their Estate Office and Guest House. The Brewers Arms was mentioned first in 1809, as the Life Boat Inn, now it is The Badgers Watch.

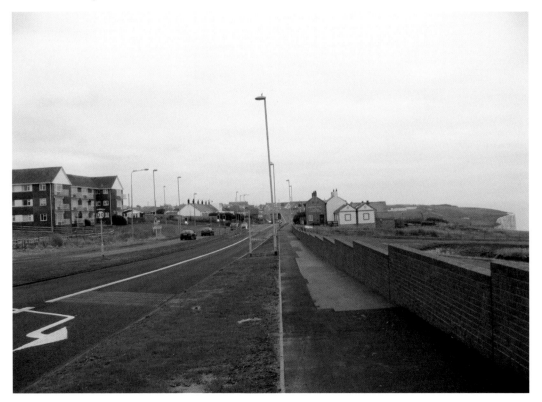

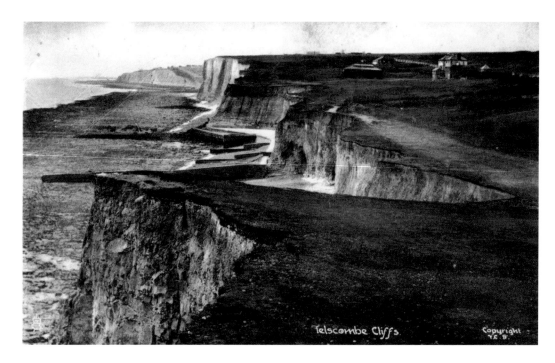

A view looking from Telscombe Cliffs back to Saltdean (which was also built up by Charles Neville) shows a coastal view before development started with just the Portobello Outfall station buildings. Portobello sewerage works came into being following the passing of 'The Brighton Intercepting and Outfall Sewers Act' of 1870.

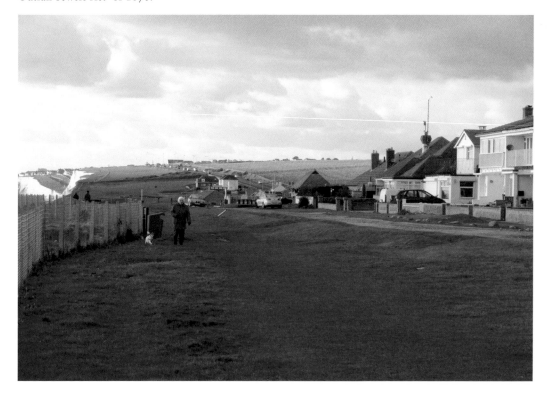

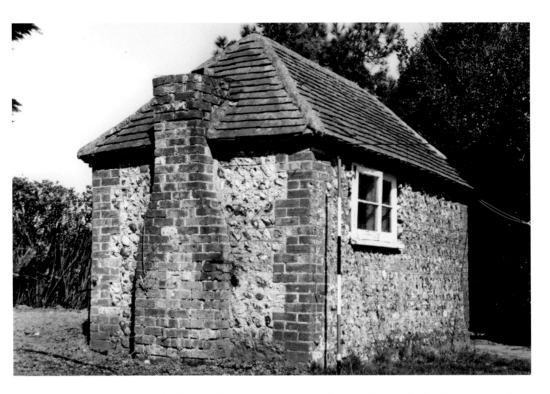

Peacehaven – the oldest building and only one that is listed is 'the Shepherds Cott', now in the front garden of house built in a newly constructed in a road only created in the 1980s.

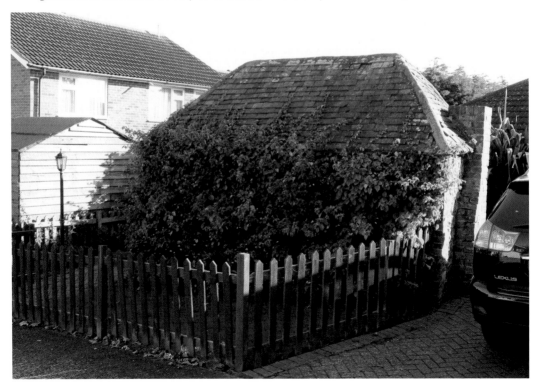

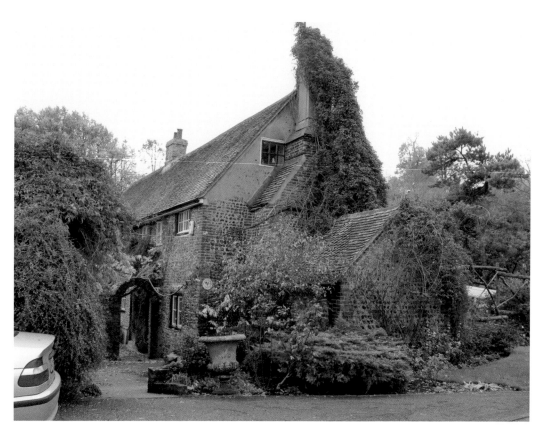

Just in Peacehaven but could be considered Piddinghoe, Halcombe Farm was recorded in ancient records of the parish, and is now a modern farm house. Once part of Hoddern Farm, there is an ancient reference in the 1086 Domesday Book to Harpingdean that could be the origin of the name.

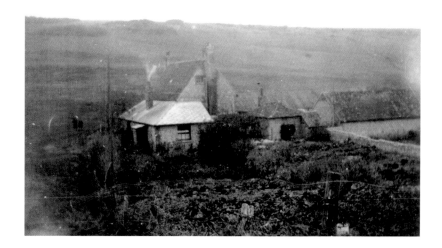

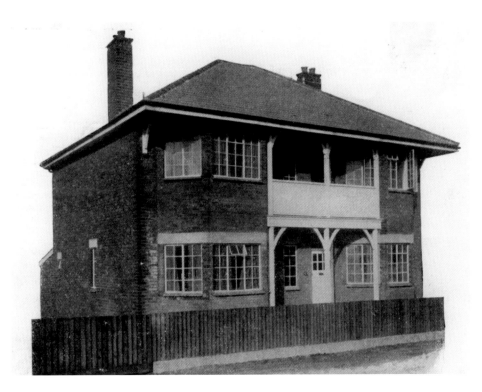

Ballater the house built for Dr Milson R. Rhodes in Phyllis Avenue was pictured in *Peacehaven Post* dated 1-3-25. It still looks the same, one of the few that is easy to recognise. He worked in practice in Manchester, then after serving during the Great War (1914–1918) as surgeon at Sea. He was medical officer to the New Zealand Prime Minister. In 1923 he moved to Steyning Avenue prior to his house in Phyllis Avenue being built.

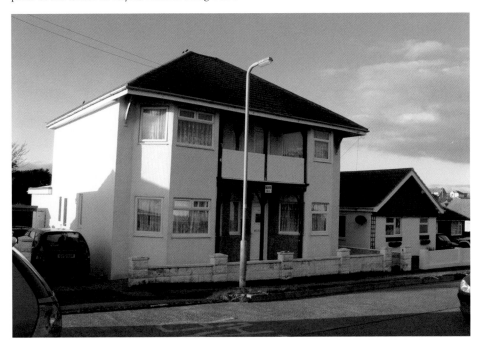

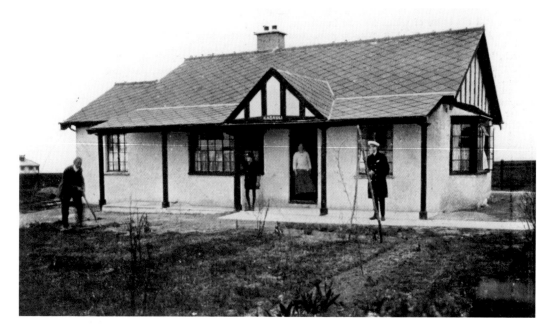

Kasauli in Cornwall Avenue, the home of Captain & Mrs W. V. Somers named after the town in India in which he served as an army officer, being inspector of Army Schools. The house was shown in the *Peacehaven Post* June 1923. He and his family retired to Peacehaven though his son is shown as a naval cadet and his daughter was a pupil at Peacehaven College.

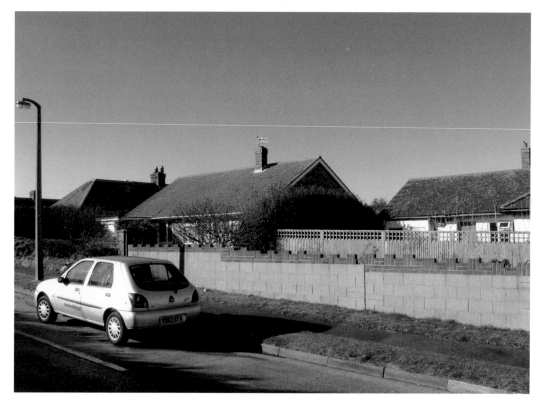

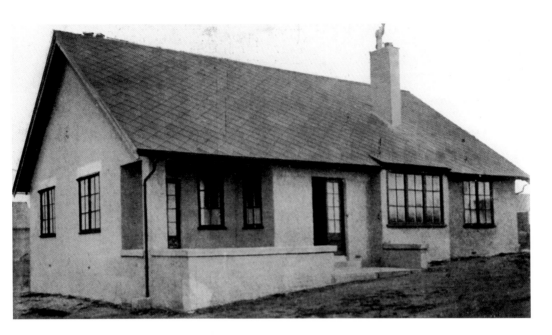

Miss James's Peacehaven College and Preparatory School as depicted in *Peacehaven Post* March 1923. The original building shown here was at the top of Victoria Avenue. She was a musician and long standing teacher, to children of Naval Officers and worked in Naval Ordnance during the First World War. Within a couple of years the college was in the hands of a Miss Golding who by the 1930s had moved the college to Arundel Road, where by the end of the decade it was a girls' school.

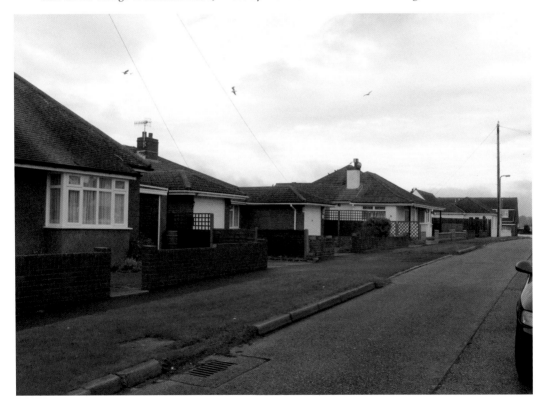

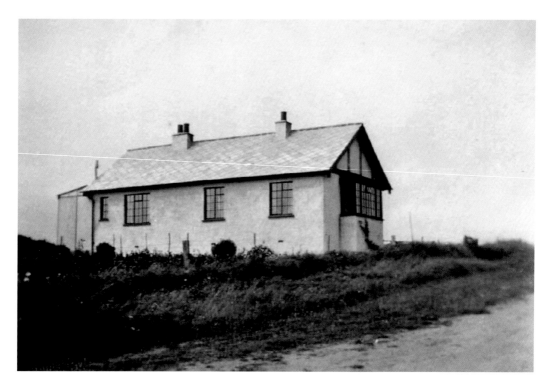

Rosemount the home of Mr & Mrs H. Selby and their daughter Bessie, in Phyllis Avenue. It would have been built in 1927 and it was only on Bessie's death in 2005 that the site was rebuilt. It is now a double property, 2 Rustic Road and 19 Downs Walk (the new name for Phyllis Avenue North).

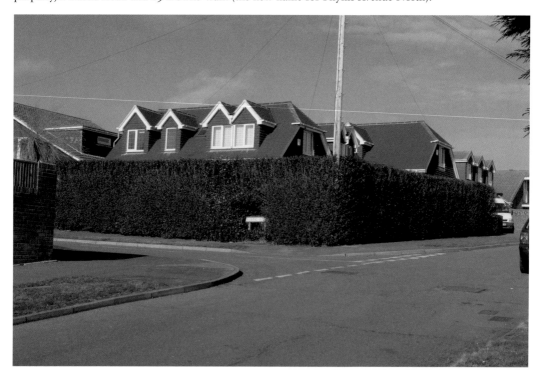

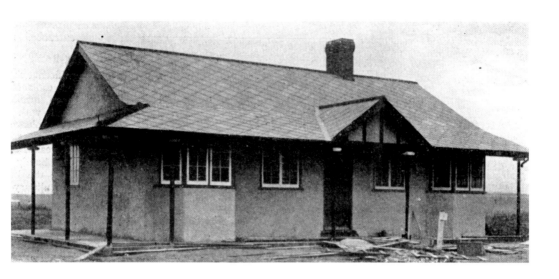

Hewley was a house picked from the design book supplied by the South Coast & Land Resort Co. to prospective purchasers. Mr H. Wigley and his wife chose a type 076 to be built for them in Keymer Avenue and moved in during April 1922. He had worked all round the world from South Africa to Panama. It appears to still be there!

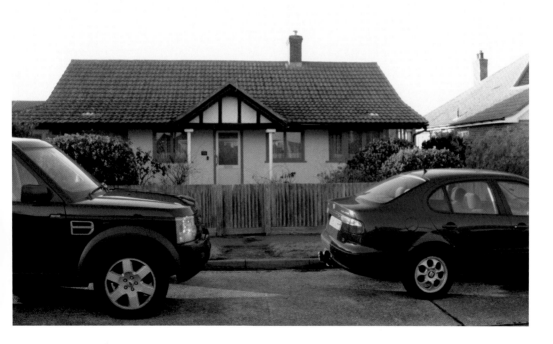

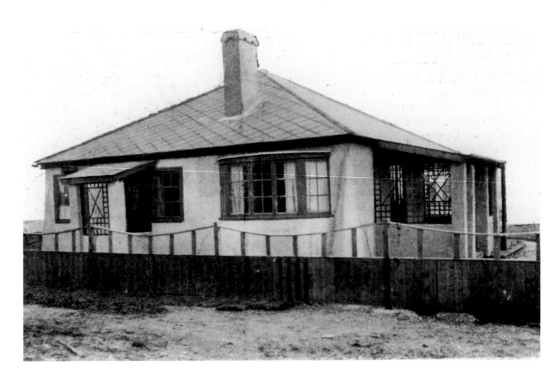

Knockdolian was described in the *Peacehaven Post* in March 1923 as 'his sweet little bungalow' and that 'in Capel Avenue near the cliffs, Dr and Mrs Moore have an unobstructed view of the channel.'

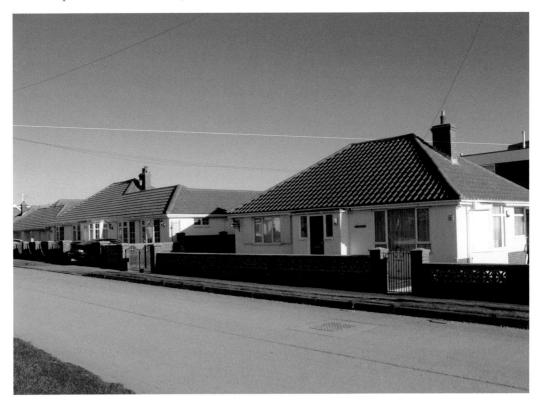

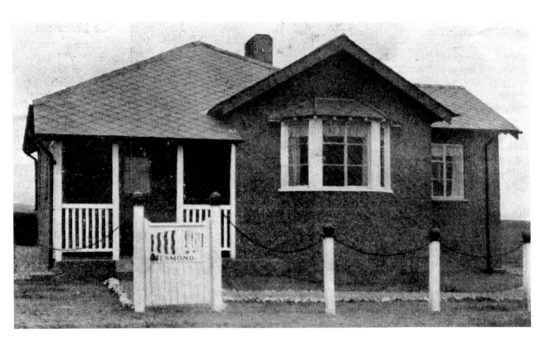

Jesmond in Southdown Avenue was built for Mr & Mrs William Shank in 1922, but we do not know what improvements were made to design 077 of the design book supplied by the company. Mr Shank was one of those who the *Peacehaven Post* used to show people who had moved to the town for health reasons. Now it is long gone.

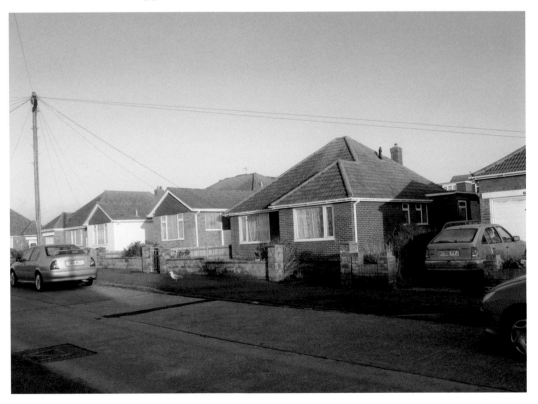

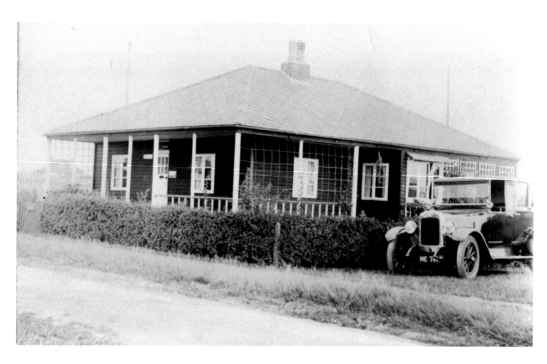

The Nook in Phyllis Avenue was the home of W. Possee in the 1920s and 30s in the card it shows he owned a car, something not everyone would have owned but there was no telephone line in the street at the time. The owner of the bungalow may have had a radio as we can see an aerial. It is another old property that was quite a way from his nearest neighbour the new bungalows in its place are close together.

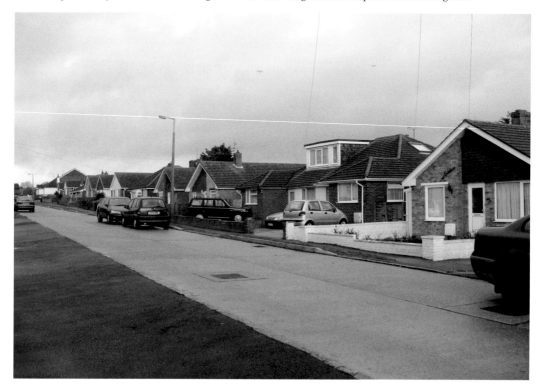

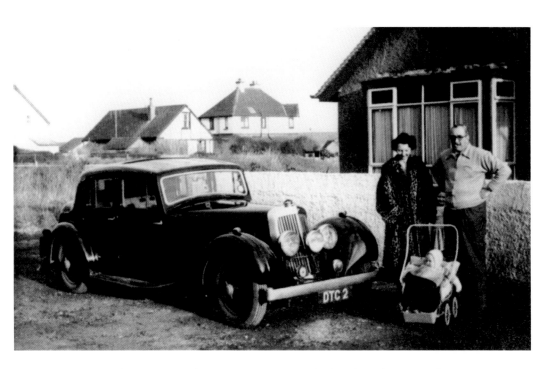

Taken in 1954 showing a proud Mr & Mrs Going outside their bungalow at 19 Slindon Avenue, with their pride and joy, a car and baby. The following year, Mr Going added a second bungalow next door at number 21. The years have passed and both have since been replaced with a more modern pair of semi-detached bungalows, and the rest of road completely built up.

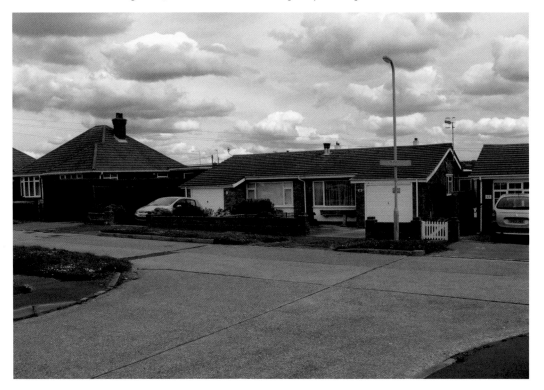

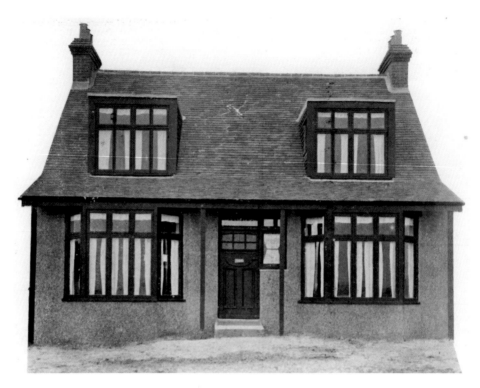

Sunnycroft in Dorothy Avenue was the home of Mr Mark C. Ord, MBE, and Miss Mary Ord a local violin teacher who played in the Peacehaven Philharmonic Societies' concerts. Mr Ord was a retired civilian engineer in the Admiralty, were he had worked for 26 years gaining his MBE for special war work in the 1914-18 conflict.

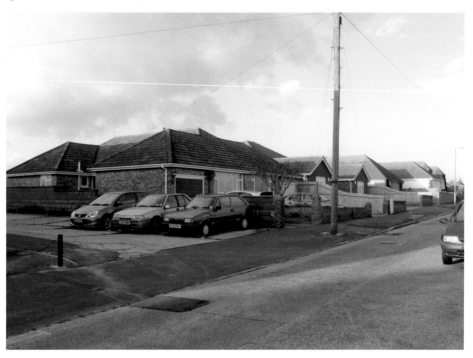

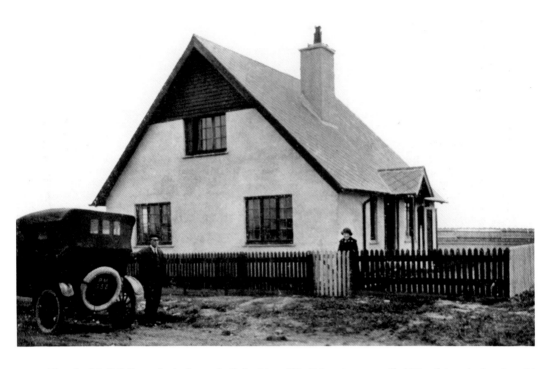

Chemist Mr T. J. Evans had a house built for himself in Friars Avenue, called 'Gwnfa', and when he sold up the bungalow was purchased by Miss A. E. Pretty.

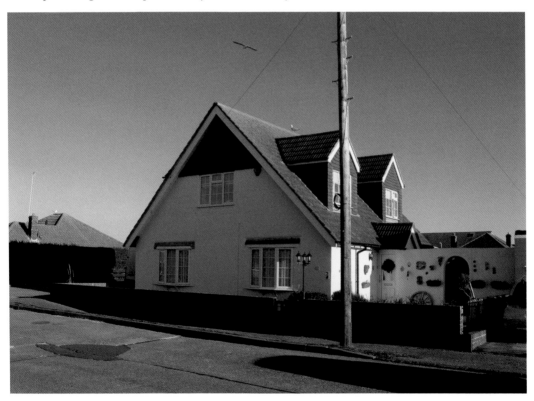

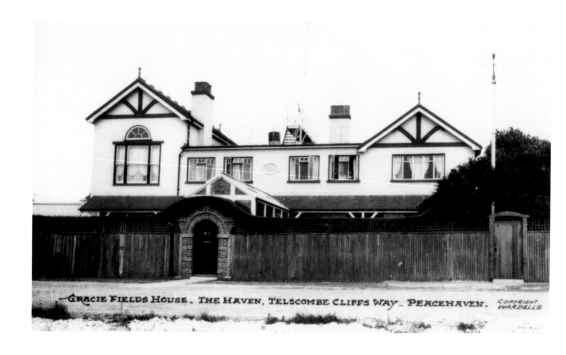

GRACIE FIELDS HOUSE - THE HAVEN, TELSCOMBE CLIFFS WAY - PEACEHAVEN. COPYRIGHT WARDELLS

The Haven was re-built in 1933 by Dame Gracie Fields (1898-1979) famous singer, star of Music Hall and film. The building in Telscombe Cliffs Way, not her first residence here, was a home for both Gracie and her parents when they moved down from Rochdale via Brighton. Today it is a care and nursing home.

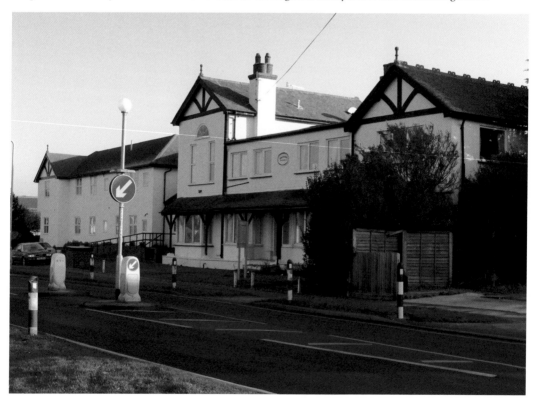

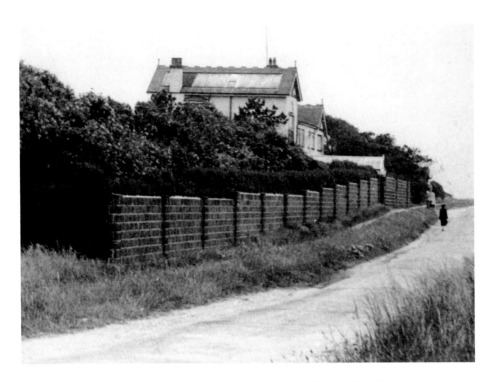

Telscombe Cliffs Way, formerly Western Avenue, is a good example of the roads in both Peacehaven and Telscombe Cliffs before the 1950s when roads were made up. Also it can be seen that the Haven was at the time quite remote with a clear view of the coast. Now it is a busy route to the houses to the north of the town.

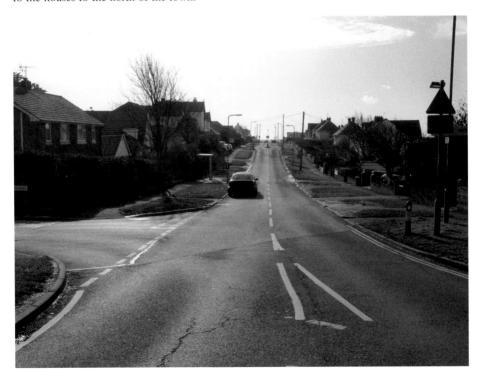

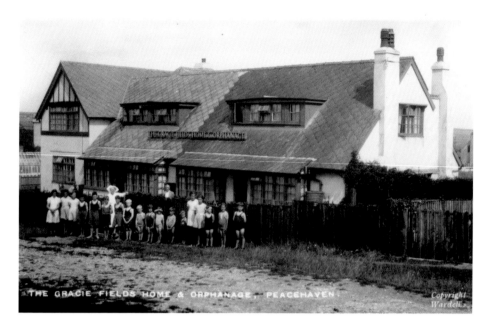

Gracie Fields owned a number of properties, the other main one was in Dorothy Avenue, bought initially for her father Fred Stansfield. She later used it for the Gracie Fields Home and Orphanage, a home where the children of stage people could be looked after. They were not orphans and many of them did not like being termed orphans. The Home was run by the Variety Artists Ladies Guild but by 1967 was losing money and closed to be taken over by the Peacehaven & Telscombe Housing Association as Dorothy House for sheltered housing.

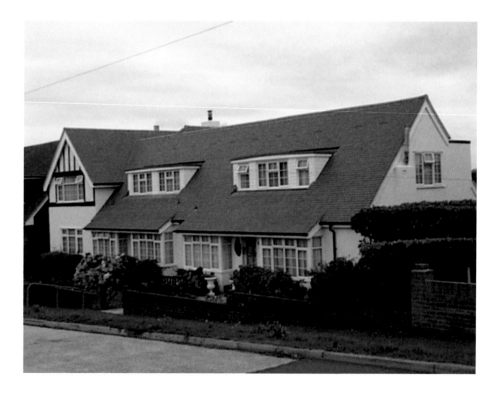

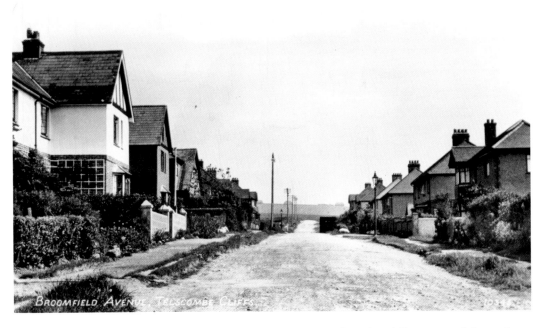

As late at as 1954 when this card of Broomfield Avenue in Telscombe Cliffs was posted the road was unmade. At this time you could then see both the downs and the sea, now though it leads to a housing estate and the busy South Coast Road.

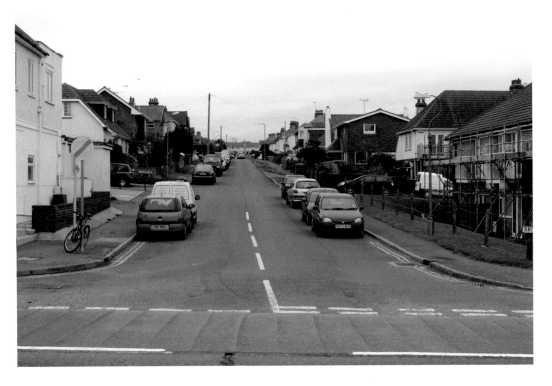

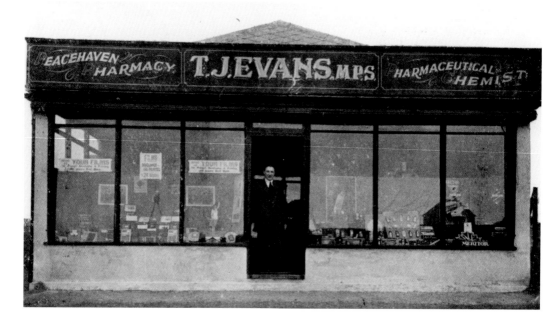

Cavell House is a shop on the South Coast Road that had started life as a department store owned by Mr Matherson (boot repairs, crested china etc). Mr T. J. Evans came in 1923, initially taking over the chemist department. In the following two years he took over the whole premises creating a modern chemist. The picture shows his name over the shop in 1926, it was taken over by A. A. Murray. Much later R. J. Williamson took over and moved the chemist across the road. Today the building is a bookmakers.

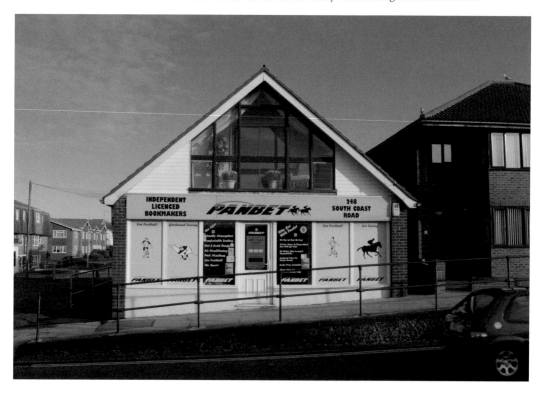

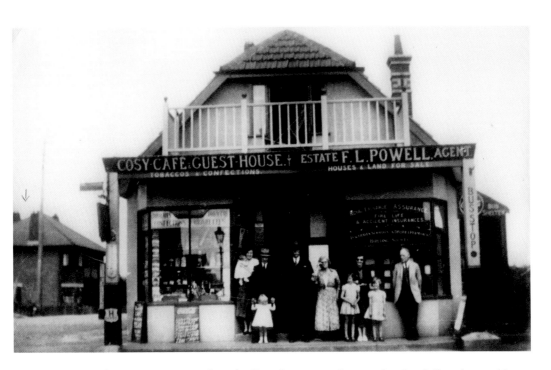

The Cosy Café was amongst a number of cafés and tea rooms that populated early Peacehaven, this one combined the trade with that of Estate Agents. The building is now a small block of flats.

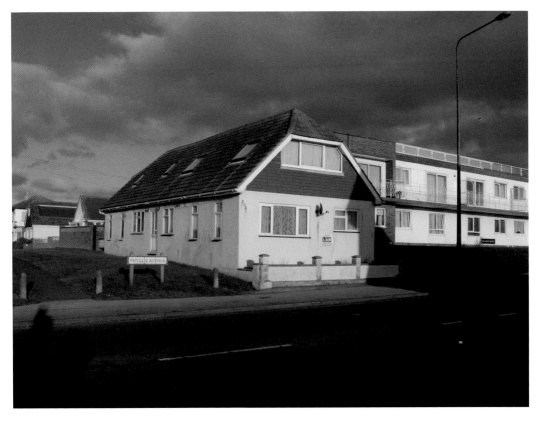

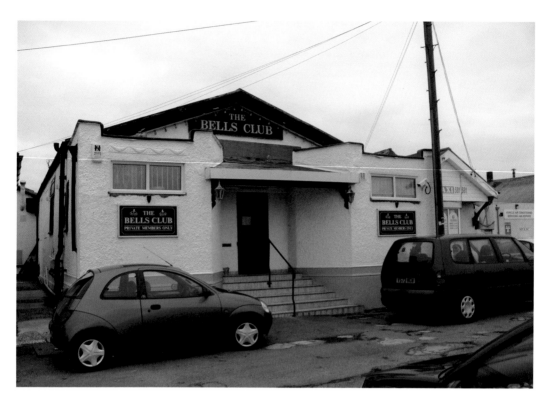

Lureland Hall was built as a dance hall opposite the Hotel Peacehaven in 1923. Besides dances, ever popular whist drives were also regularly held. Today it is the Bells Club.

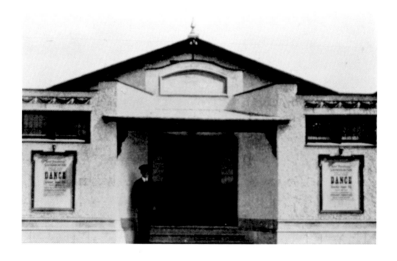

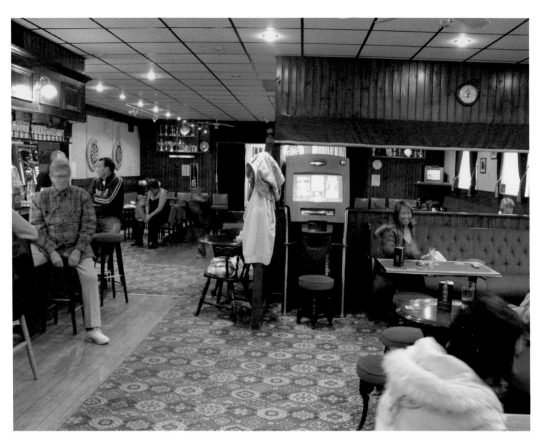

Lureland Hall was popular for dances for many years as well as many community meetings. Today as the Bells Club it has a less formal atmosphere and a more user friendly layout as a club.

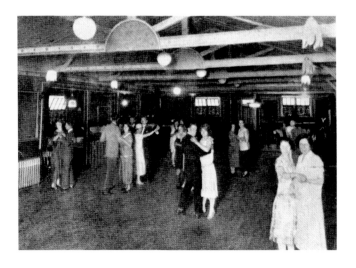

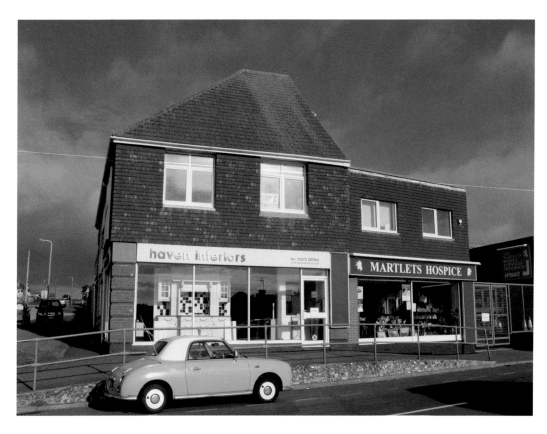

Mr G. E. Buck opened his confectionery and tobacconist store in 1923, it even had a petrol dispenser outside for cigarette lighters! In 1933 Mr King took over the premises, Much later after the end of the Second World War (1939-1945) Bob Poplett took over the premises as an ironmongers and builders merchants. Bob, one time town councillor, was a local historian who died towards the end of 2008.

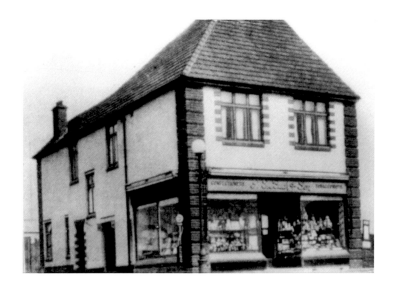

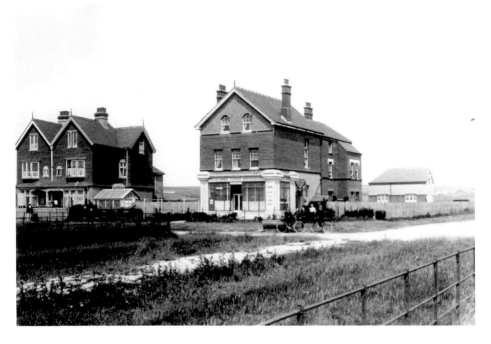

A building now replaced by Telscombe Town Council Offices, had a long and varied career. It started life as the Estate Office of the Cavendish Land Co. Ltd. The building served in 1903 as restaurant, boarding house and Estate Agents. In the 1920s South Coast Land & Resort Company took over and it then became the Western Estate Office, finally becoming the Cliffs Club, before being rebuilt.

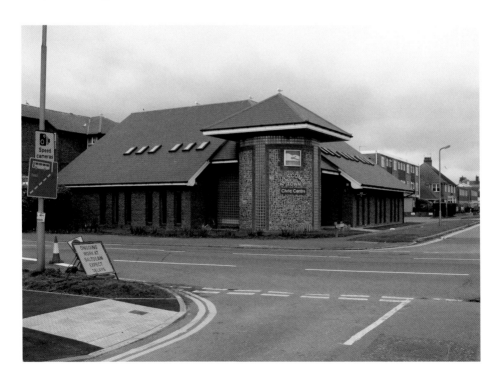

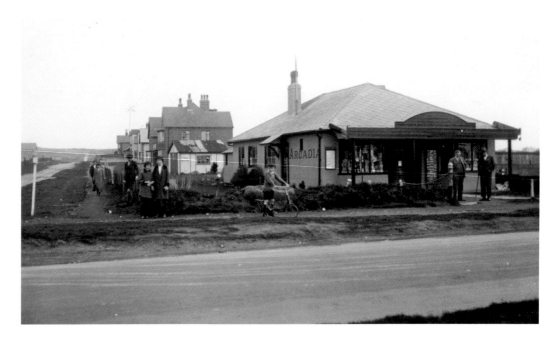

Arcadia Stores was opened by the enterprising Mr Parker who in 1923 sold his Optima Stores in Peacehaven to open Arcadia Stores at the corner of Central Avenue on the other side of the road to the Estate Office. A few years later he sold this business to Mr Gamblin, it was a very busy Post Office right through to 2002 when it closed for good, later it was pulled down and the site rebuilt.

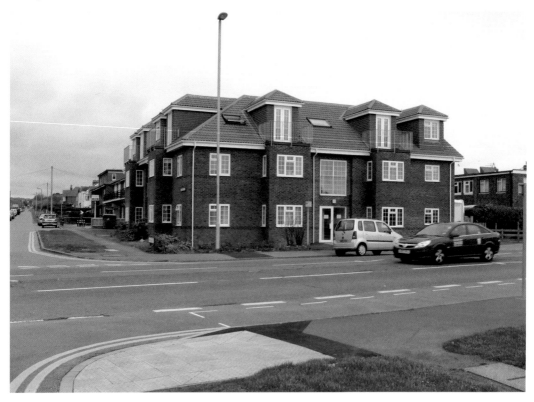

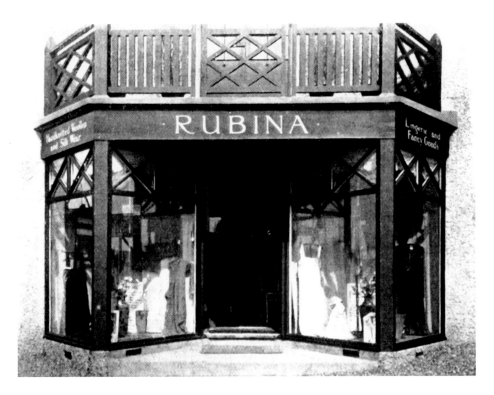

Rubina run by Miss Garnham and Miss Drew as a lingerie and fancy goods shop and a type of fashion clothing called Modes in the directories of the late 1920s. In more recent years the building was a plumbers' merchants and more recently an antique dealers.

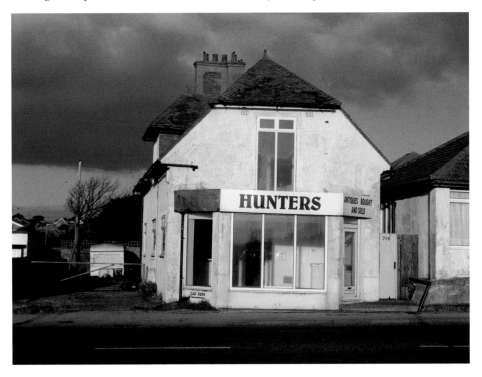

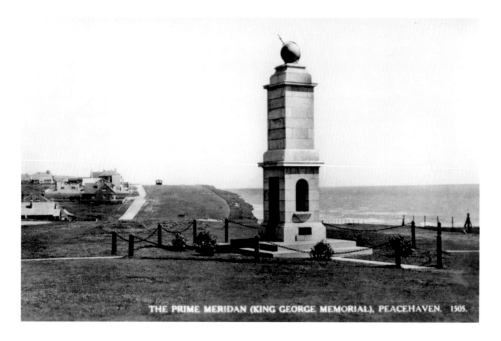

THE PRIME MERIDAN (KING GEORGE MEMORIAL), PEACEHAVEN. 1505.

The Meridian Monument was opened to a great fanfare, in 1936, originally dedicated to celebrate the silver jubilee of King George V and Queen Mary, but the king had died before it was completed. Therefore it was renamed King George V Memorial and Prime Meridian Obelisk. It was moved back from the cliff edge in the 1980s by being dismantled and rebuilt 30 feet (about 9 metres) north from the cliff edge.

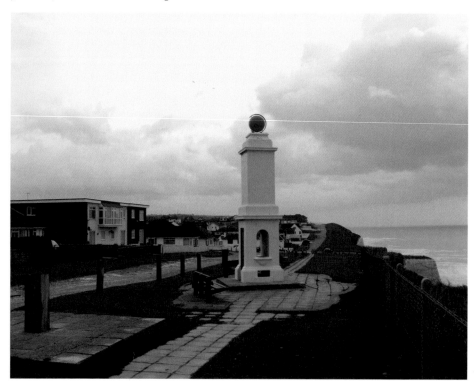

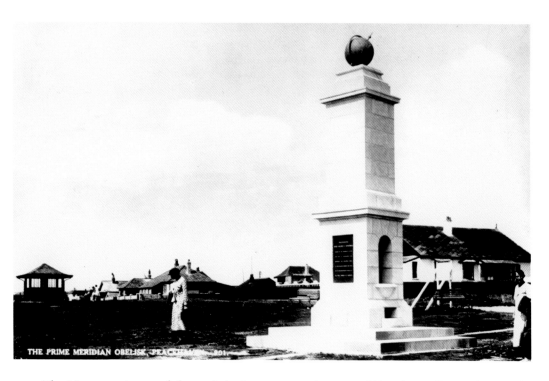

THE PRIME MERIDIAN OBELISK, PEACEHAVEN 1931

The Monument is one of the symbols that represent the town of Peacehaven. It was Commander Davenport who instigated the Prime Meridian Obelisk, having checked with the Astronomer Royal that the town stood on the Prime Meridian. The monument was moved back from the cliff edge in 1981, and the globe had to be replaced after the great storm of 1986.

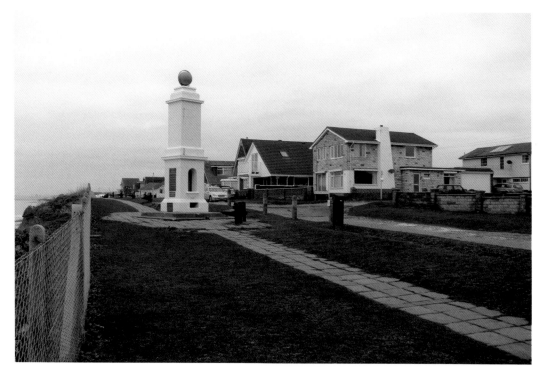

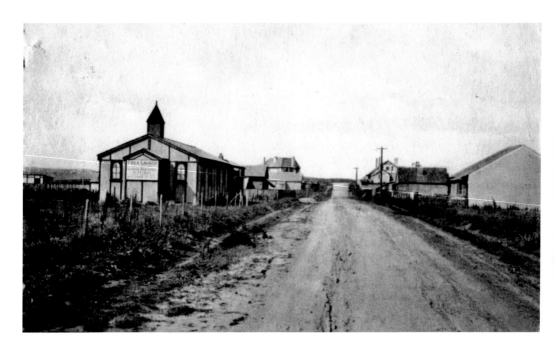

Peacehaven from its earliest days had many churches, according to the 1925/26 directory there were five serving the fledgling community. The Evangelical Free Church shown here was in Mayfield Avenue an unmade road as usual. The modern church has moved to the South Coast Road, with the site of the original building used as a community hall, which can just be seen in the background.

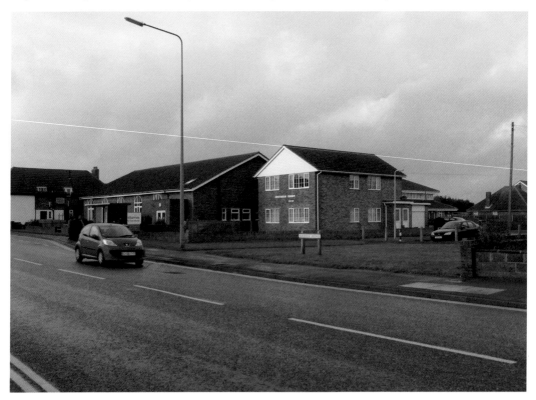

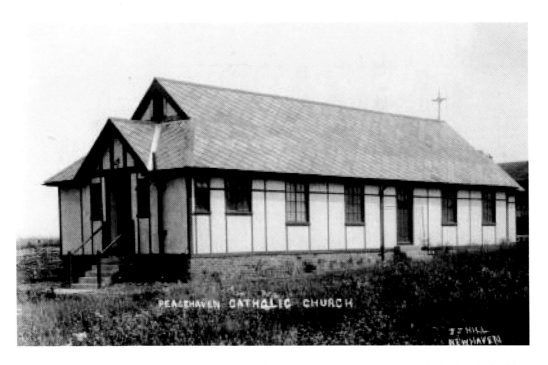

The Catholic Church in Edith Avenue started life as a more temporary structure, which after the building of the current church, was used for many years as a church hall until it finally was pulled down.

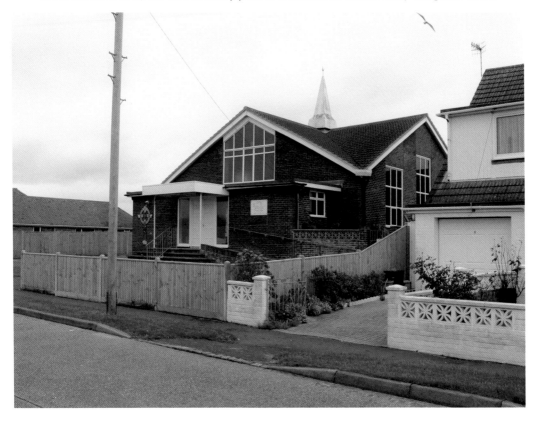

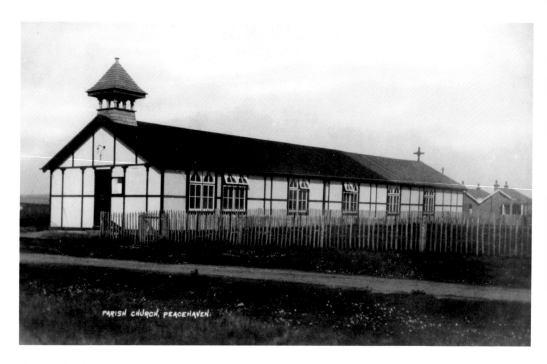

The Parish Church (C of E) shown as the temporary building of the 1920s, between Steyning Avenue and Bramber Avenue along Arundel Road an area at the time towards the centre of the growing town. A brick built church was not designed and built until the mid 1950s, the site also houses Peacehaven's war memorial.

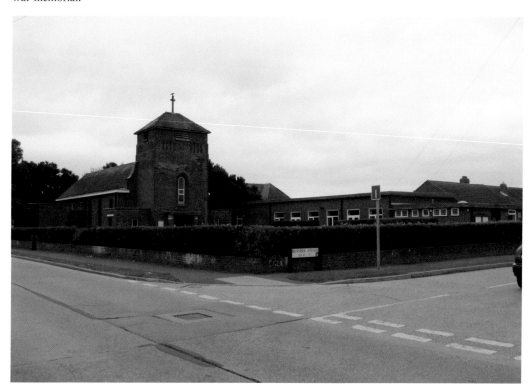

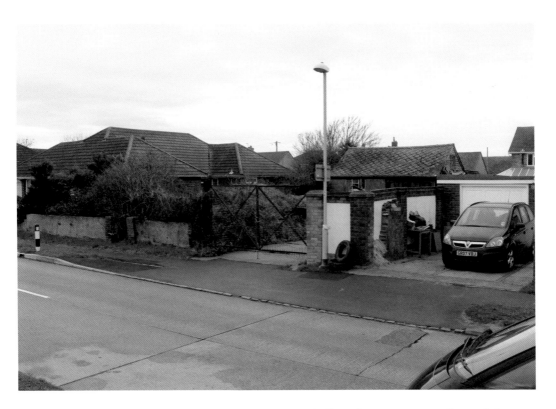

Bronte in Seaview Avenue, was the original house and office of Mr Isaac Wagstaff one of the true pioneers of the town. In 1929 he moved to the South Coast Road, however part of his old workshop still exists beside the bungalows that were developed on the site in the 1970s. Jack his son is noted as the first child to have been born in the town.

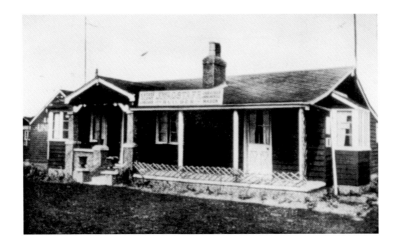

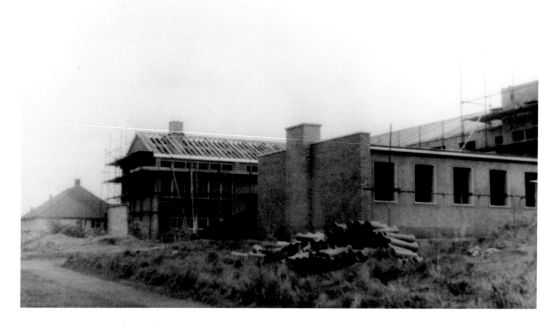

Hoathdown House in Cissbury Avenue, on what was Friars Bay Estate started off as 'The Tin School' opened in September 1926 closing in 1938. The site was rebuilt in 1961 as Hoathdown House by the County Council's welfare services department they later renamed the building as Downlands. It has since closed again with plans for an extra care housing scheme approved in 2007 and work started late in 2008.

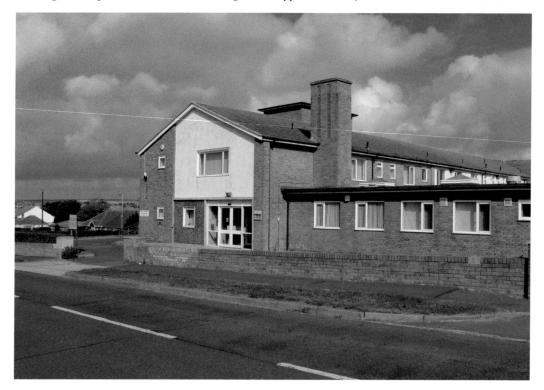

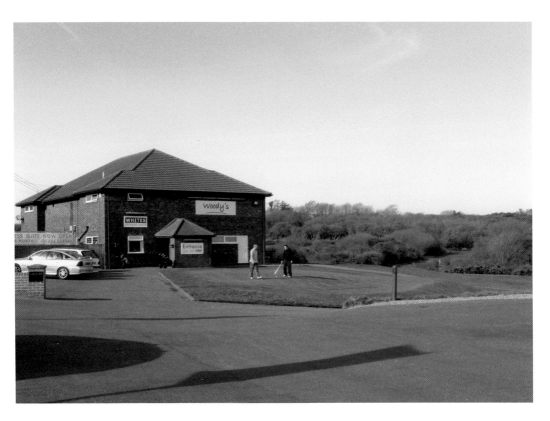

At the far end of Peacehaven almost in Newhaven is the Peacehaven Golf Club, once in the middle of nowhere, is now a thriving centre with a modern Club House.

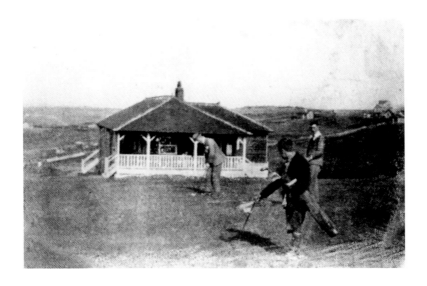

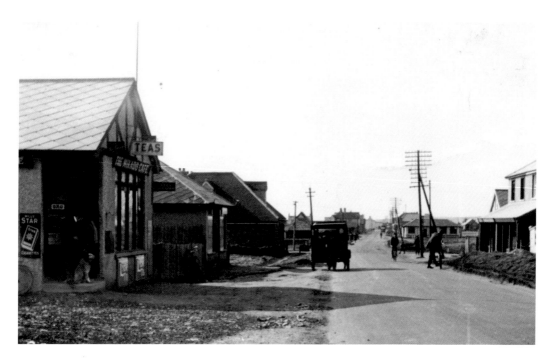

Peacehaven in its early days was the home of the tea room; according to the 1925/26 Peacehaven Directory there were thirteen. Mikado run by Mrs Simpkins was at the corner of South Coast Road and Vernon Avenue. In the early 1930s it was taken over by Miss F. Hilton, the old tea rooms have all gone now.

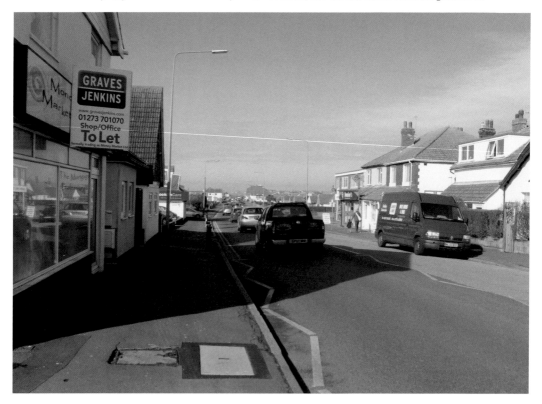

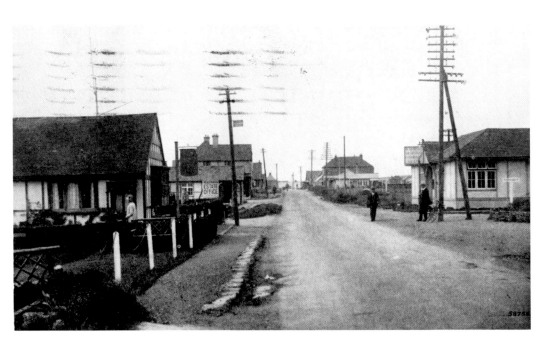

The Rosemary Tea Room was formerly the Estate Office which the company moved slightly further down the road in 1922 as can be seen in the picture. The Rosemary was a popular tea room that was started by Mr and Mrs T. E. Thornton it even included a large room with a piano, in its place today is a block of terraced houses.

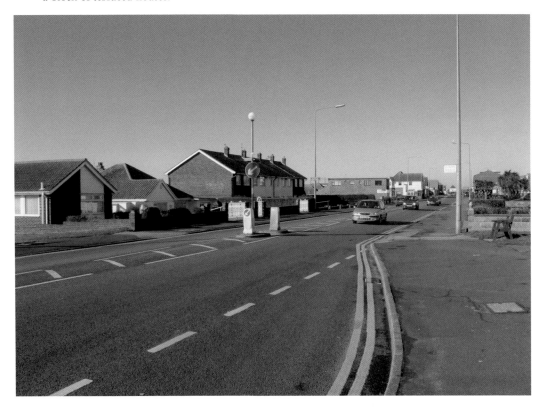

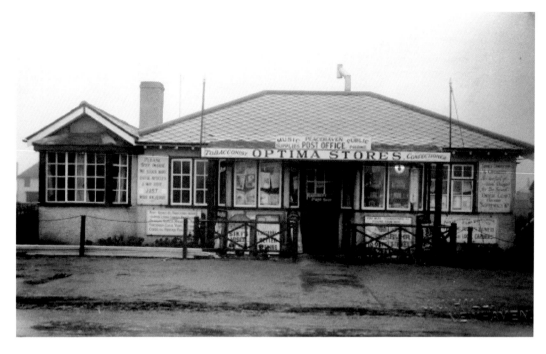

Along the Coast Road towards Newhaven, you came across Mr Parker's original Optima Stores, although by the time this picture was taken it may have been owned by Mr Greenwood. The stores, although remodelled, is still a post office. In 1921 it became a sub-Post Office and had one of the earliest telephones, its initial phone number was Newhaven 10.

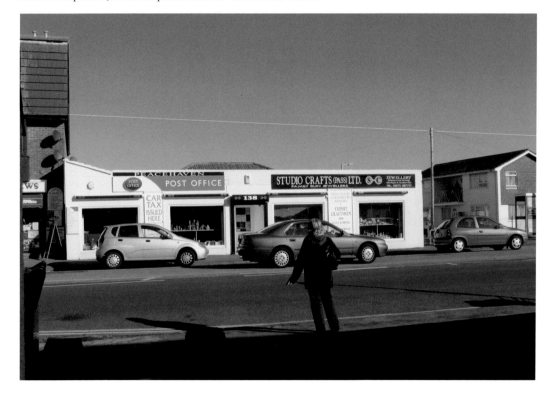

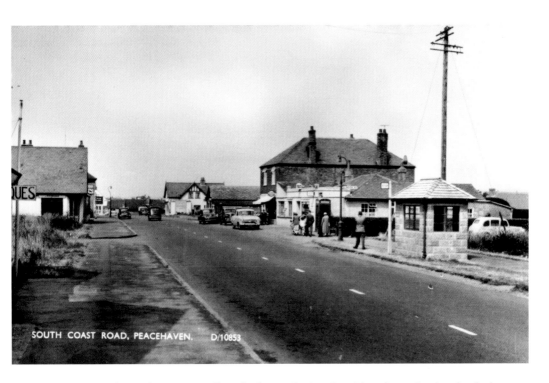

SOUTH COAST ROAD, PEACEHAVEN. D/10853

The area around Peacehaven Post Office (the former Optima Store) has changed quite a lot the bus stop had to move to make way for the pedestrian crossing. However more dramatic are the shops next door which were constructed in 1986 and next to that block is the latest change beginning in 2008 another new building went up in place of an old land mark.

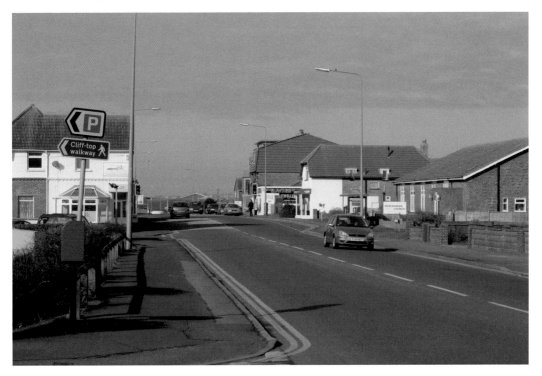

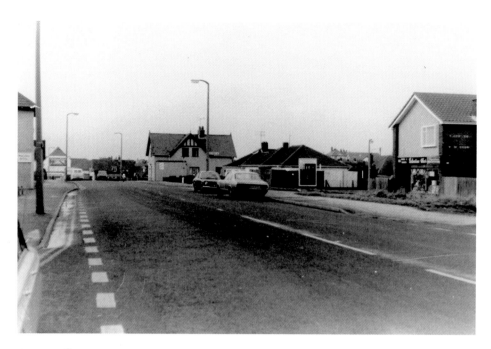

Starting off as Pioneer Stores a new store for Mr A. J. O'Dell in the early 1920s later taken over by Mr F. Burden who modernised the off licence. In the 1960s, the picture shows the rebuilt store then owned by Valentine Charles. In more recent years the business was run as Roy's Liquor Store and in 2008 Roy's moved next door and again the whole building has been pulled down and we are yet to see who moves in.

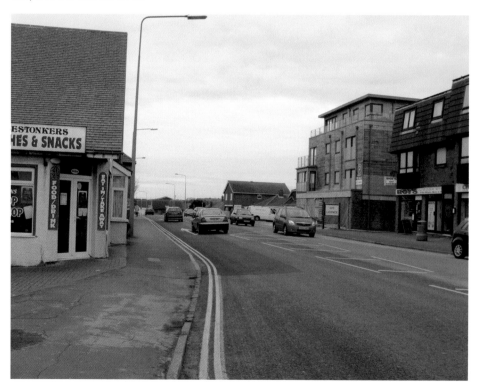

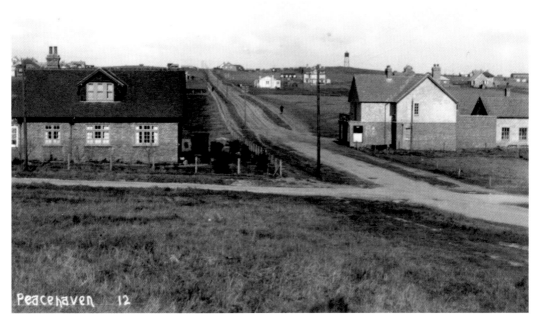

Inland from the Coast Road the main road was Roderick Avenue, but if you lived here in the 1920s, 1930s and possibly through to the 1950s you were in the country, no made up roads and houses scattered among the plots that were never taken up. After the councils took charge from the 1950s onwards, much of the land was compulsory purchased and the north of the town could be said to be one big housing estate.

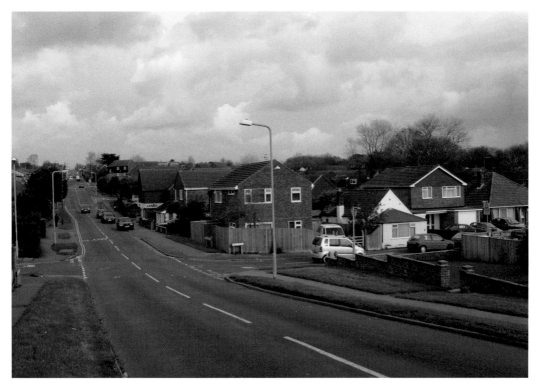

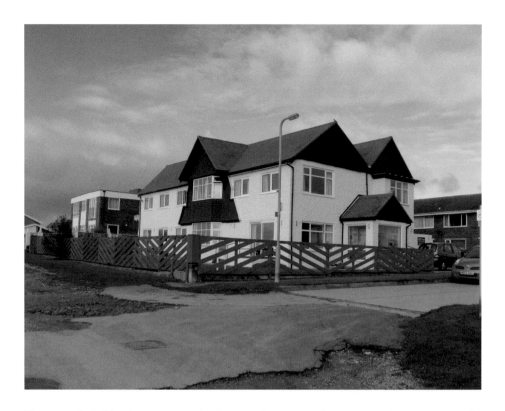

The more desirable plots were on the Promenade, Pimpernel in Keymer Avenue was on the Promenade. Owned by Mr Blakeney Pizzey, who followed Charles Nevilles example developing part of Peacehaven Heights as Blakeney Estate. Today his house has been converted and extended to become Cliffs Court Nursing Home.

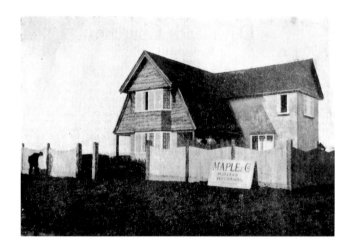

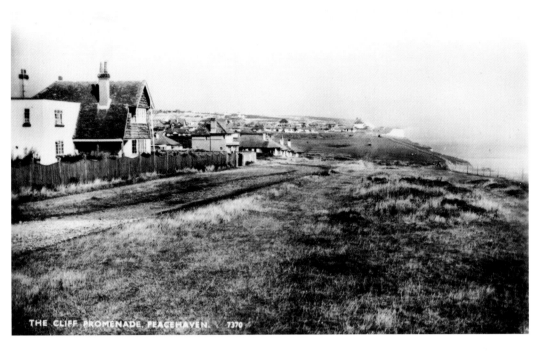

The promenade in front of Pimpernel has greatly receded, with the pathway in front now at the cliff edge. While in the original picture there is plenty of grass on the cliff top for people to picnic on.

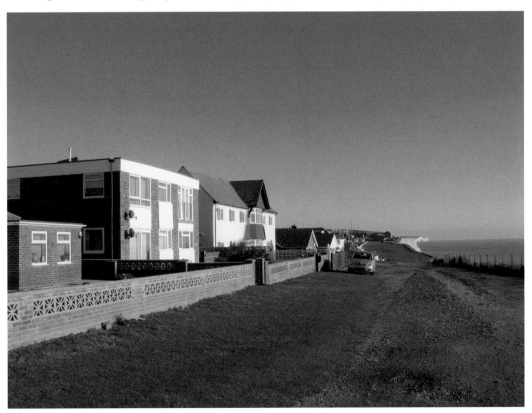

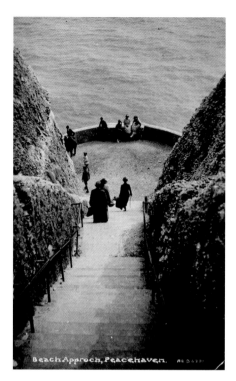

Beach Approch, Peacehaven.

The Bastion Steps a little further along the Promenade at the bottom of Steyning Avenue were very popular as there was a beach pool constructed in the 1930s for safe bathing, but this was demolished after the war. The new steps are in addition to a slope that winds its way in a large curve down to the under cliff walk.

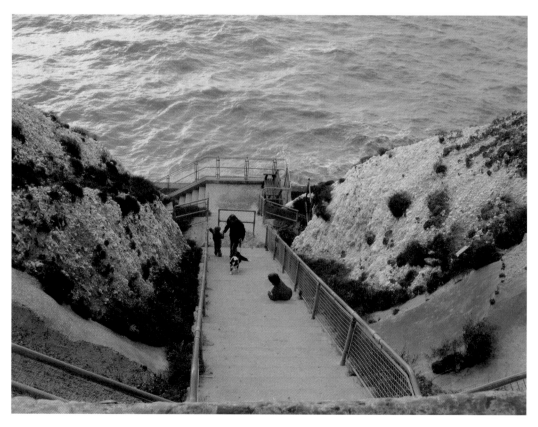

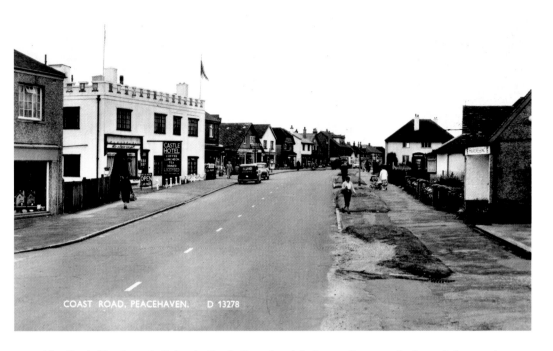

The Castle Hotel was built by the South Coast Land & Resort Company, had a varied career, but was mainly a restaurant in the 1930s and 1950s, but later became the Retreat. As the White Schooner it had a major rebuild around 2003. Funnell's the bakers just past the White Schooner was even more recently rebuilt, modernising that part of the Coast Road.

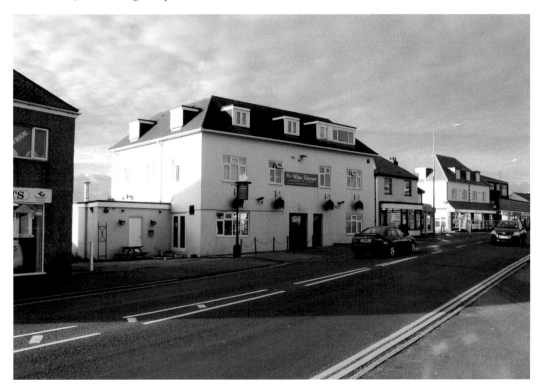

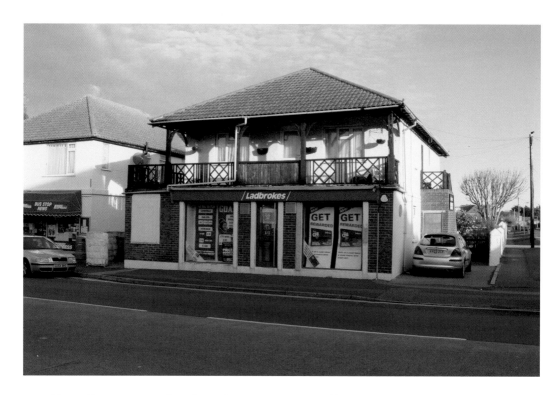

Kenya House opposite the White Schooner was so named by Mr Barker in the 1920s when he took over the restaurant having returned to Britain from Kenya. The rear of the building was later converted to the Central Club which has continued since 1929, while the front became a bookmakers.

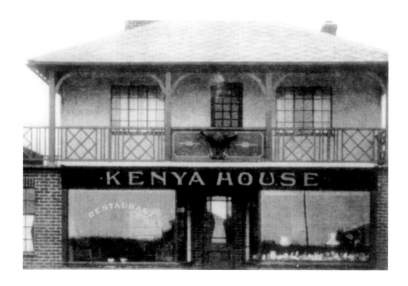

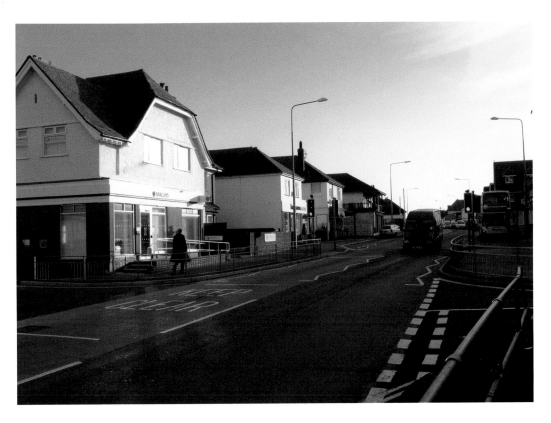

Barclays Bank moved from their temporary home in 1923 to new premises that are still there today. Although the A259 is wider and busier road today the new picture could only be taken early one Sunday morning without a continuous stream of traffic.

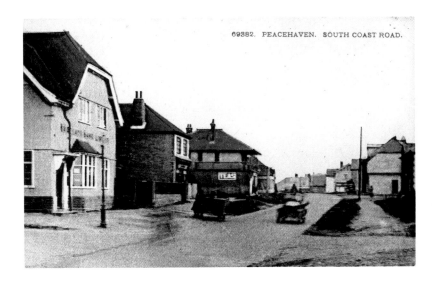

69382. PEACEHAVEN. SOUTH COAST ROAD.

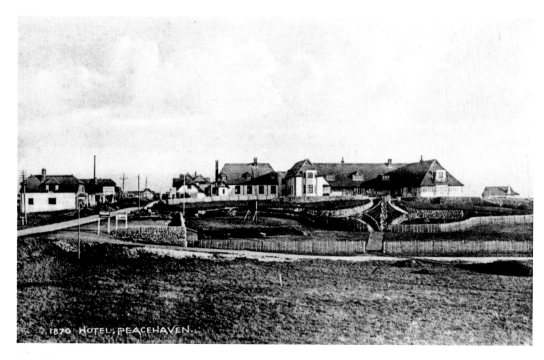

Hotel Peacehaven was opened in October 1922, with great celebration as the final triumph of Charles Neville with a sunken Italian garden, electric light throughout and hot and cold water in each room. It was finally demolished in 1987 having been derelict for a number of years. The Peacehaven Toby was later built on the site and was renamed 'The Peacehaven' at the end of December 2008.

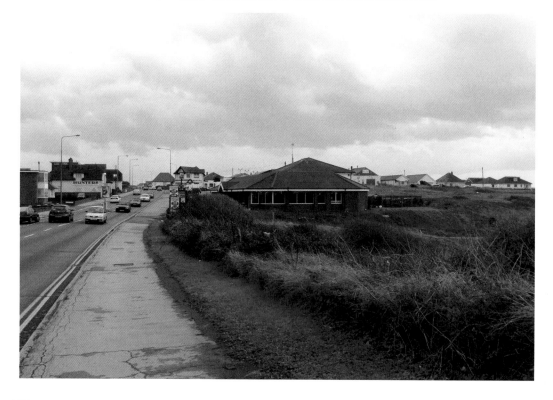

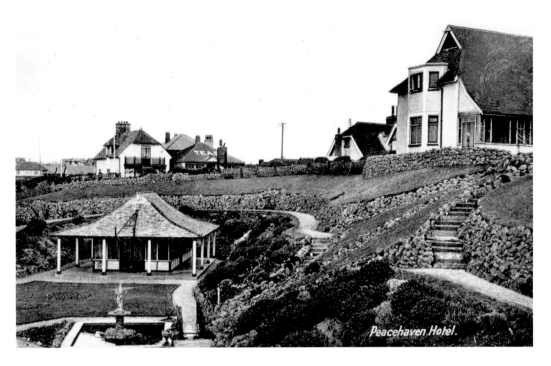

Looking from the Sunken Garden in the Hotel, just visible is Rubina on the South Coast Road. The view today is from what is now called Howard Park and you can see The Peacehaven Carvery to the right and across the road Cairo House which is now a private residence.

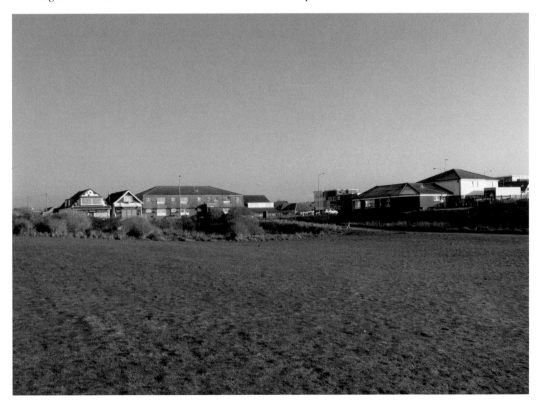

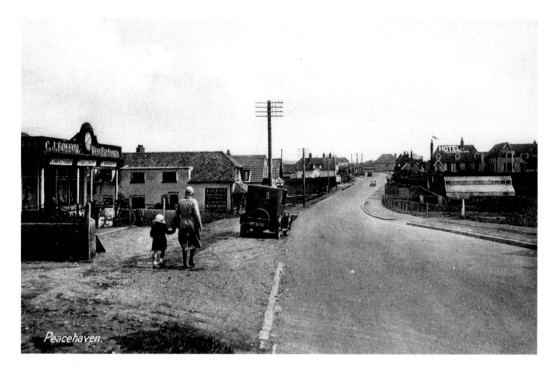

West End Stores, at the corner of Lincoln Avenue and the South Coast Road was opened by Mr J. Blewett as the first shop in at the western end of Peacehaven. This picture shows the proprietor as C. J. Bossom who first appeared as owner in the 1933 directory. Today it is Lincoln Court.

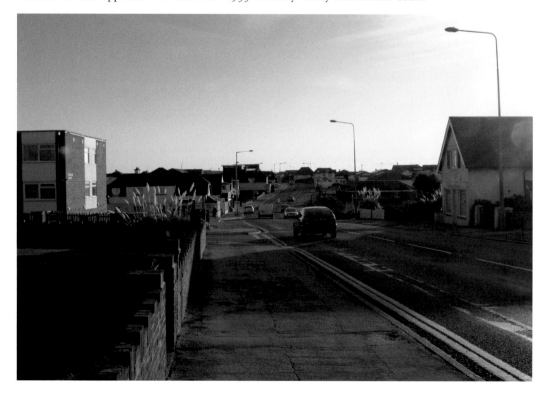

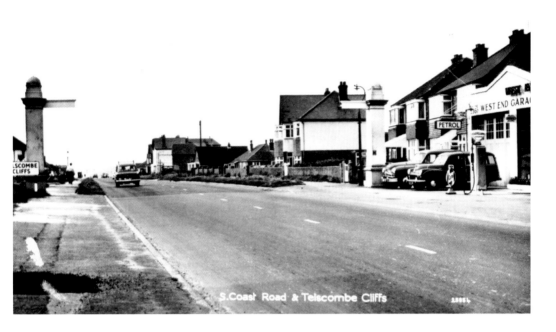

West End Garage the other side of Lincoln Avenue to West End Stores is a rare picture as is shows both pylons that welcomed visitors to Peacehaven. It closed down as a Total Garage just a couple of years ago and all that remains today, is a vacant building plot.

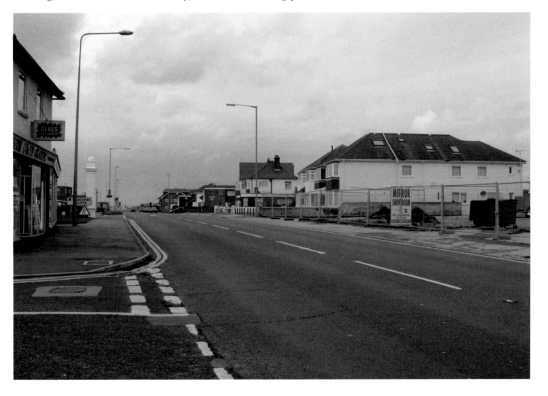

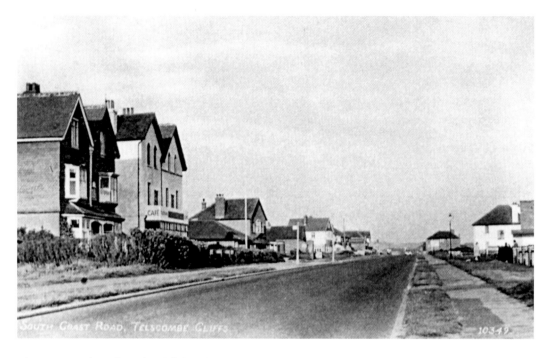

The Coast Road at Telscombe Cliffs has changed quite a lot since this picture was taken, the café on the left was the Cliffs Club now replaced by the new Civic Centre and the former Post Office has also gone to be replaced by flats. Even the road layout has recently had a make over with the installation of a bus lane.

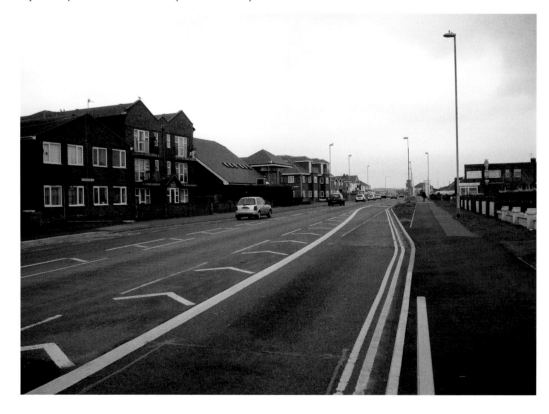

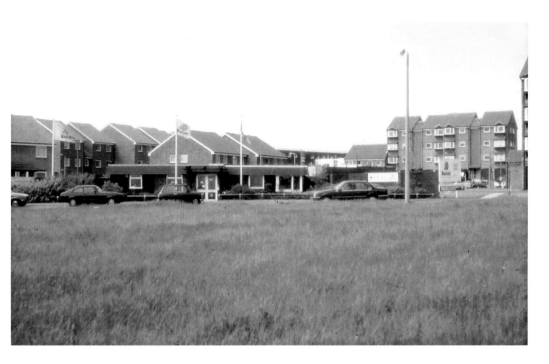

Peacehaven changed quite a lot in 1986 and possibly someone from East Sussex County Council took some pictures. This one shows Lake Park being developed by Barratt Homes, the sales hut in front was later used by the Bowls Club as a club house.

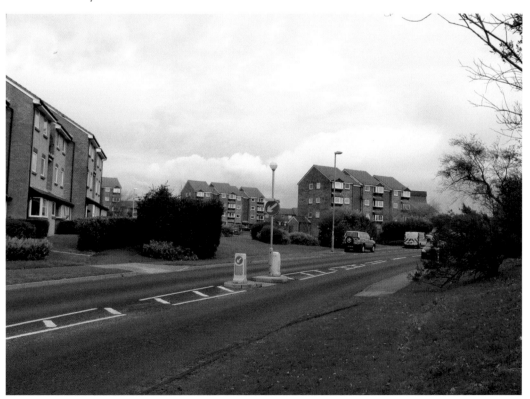

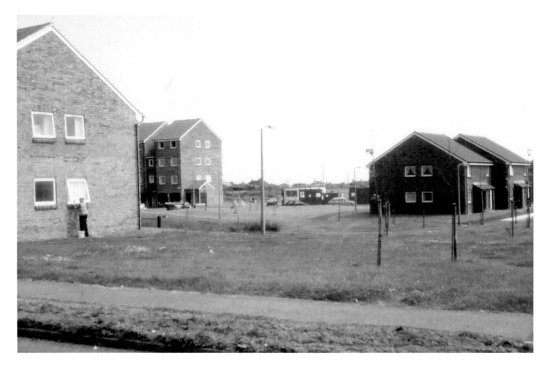

A 1986 view of the newly constructed Balcombe Court looking towards Lake Drive. The building hut for the Lake Drive flats can be seen, now the area is mature and landscaped.

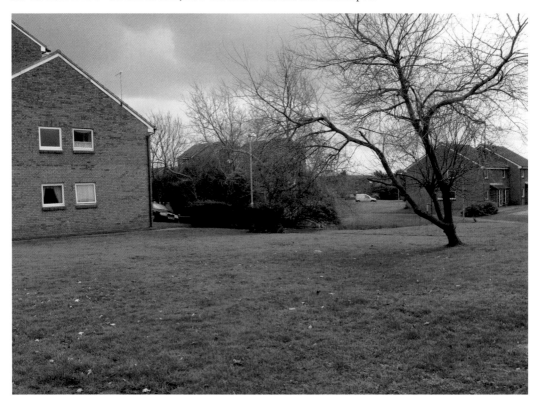

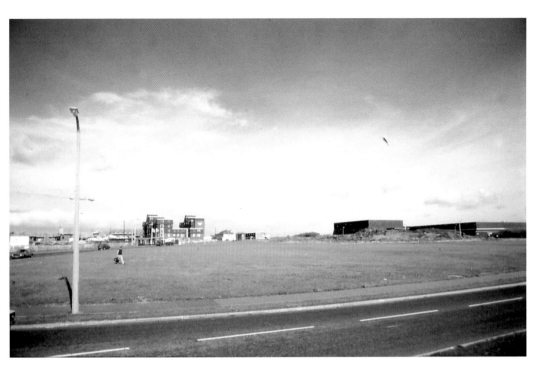

Taken in 1986, from Greenwich Way back to the new Lake Drive development and Balcombe Court. Today there is a tree-lined park on the green space in front of the southern end of the Meridian Centre.

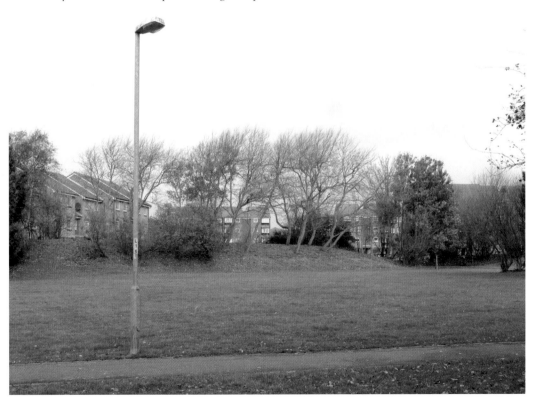

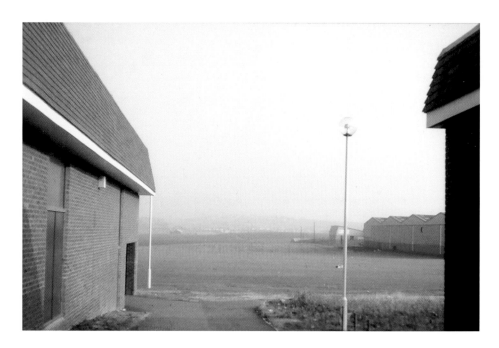

This rear back door view in 1986 shows an empty field, the left side of the Meridian Centre was for while a DIY store, today it is Peacehaven Library. To the right is now Greenwich House currently used by the mental health part of the local primary health trust. What was a green field is now Peacehaven Community School (11 to 16 year olds) which was opened in 2001, with a leisure centre next to it.

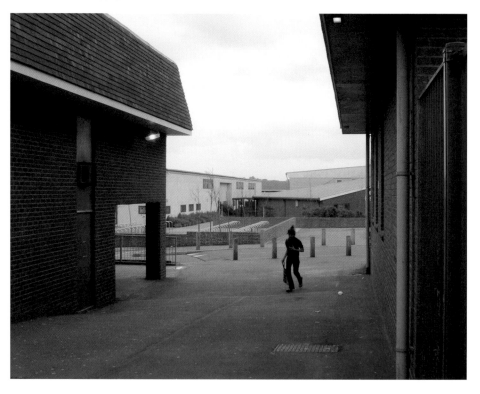

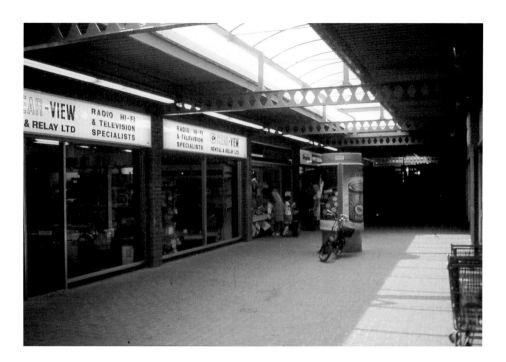

Opened in 1979, the Meridian Centre shown in 1986, this view looking south shows shops that were able to compete with the Co-op at the time, a TV and radio retailer, greengrocer and off licence. Today, Martin's occupies a prominent place opposite an expanded Co-op. The Centre was recently taken over by the Co-op who in 2008 carried out a major modernisation.

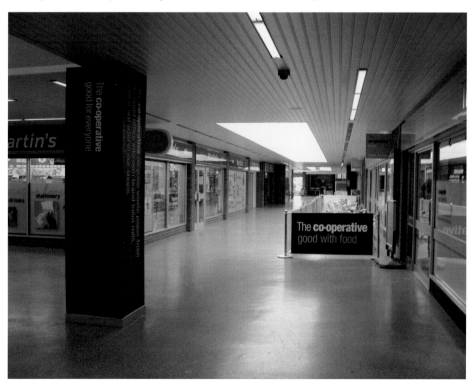

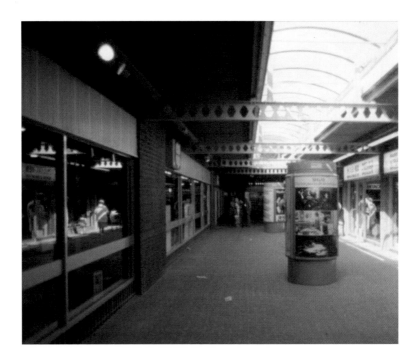

Looking north in 1986 we can see the Meridian Centre. Even though it was still new it was a
dull place dominated by the iron girders that formed the construction. The 2008 modernisation
appears to have made it a more vibrant place.

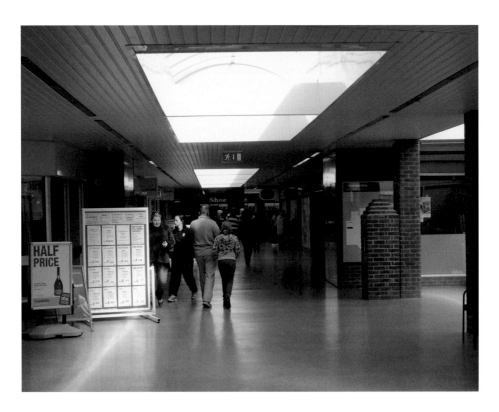

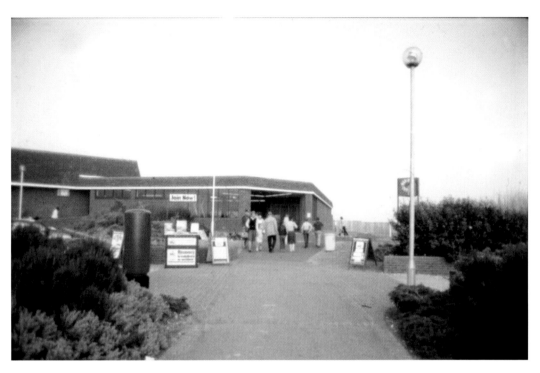

The southern entrance in 1986 sported a pillar box which has been moved inside, and the landscaping is much more mature now.

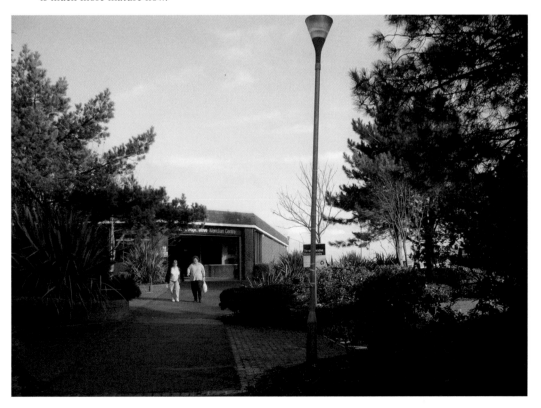

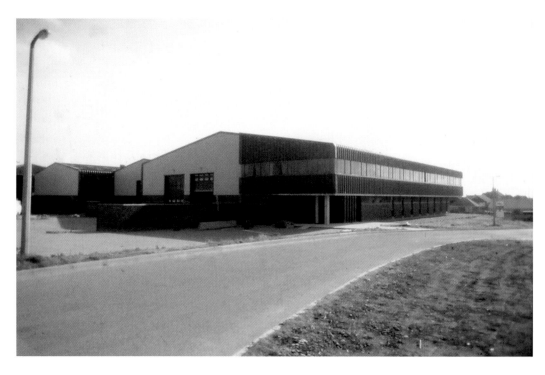

In 1986 the business units to the east of the Meridian Centre were new and this one was about to be opened then as a Co-op Homebase. That has gone and the unit along with the rest are used as light industrial units.

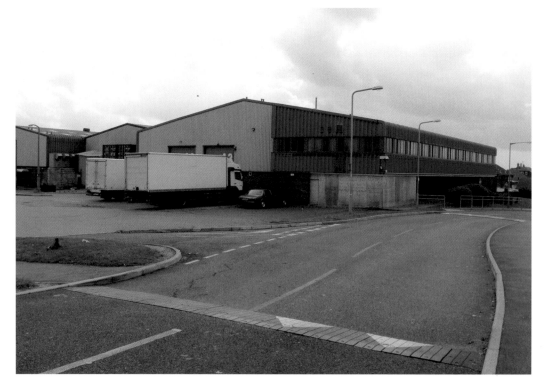

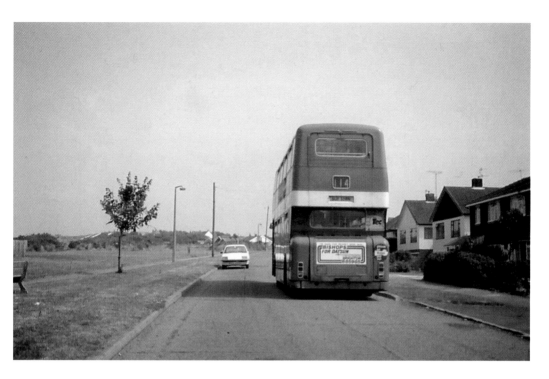

One road that has little changed since 1986, is Ambleside Avenue, though the buses are now run by Brighton and Hove Bus Company.

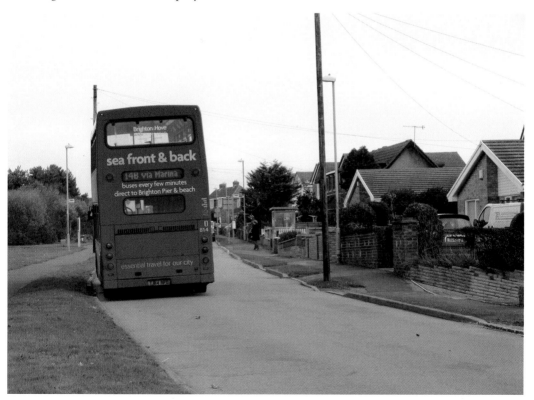

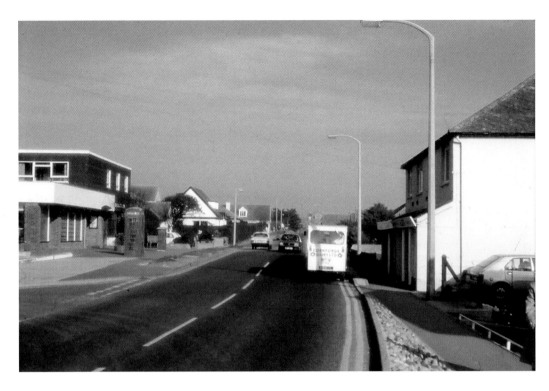

Fortunately this 1986 picture has survived as it shows a Cornford's Dairy's milk float travelling down Roderick Avenue just passing the McKellar public house. The Cornford's Dairy has now closed and the public house is now called the Good Companions and the two shops where the milk float is parked are now flats.

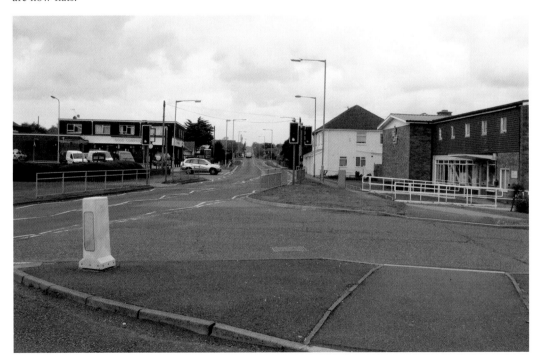

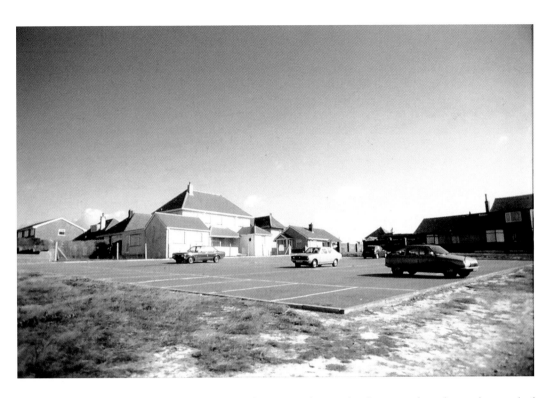

Health and safety in 1986 was not to the fore as can be seen by the car park at the southern end of Cavell Avenue as it had no fencing. The car park leads on to the southern part of the Dell open space overlooking the cliffs.

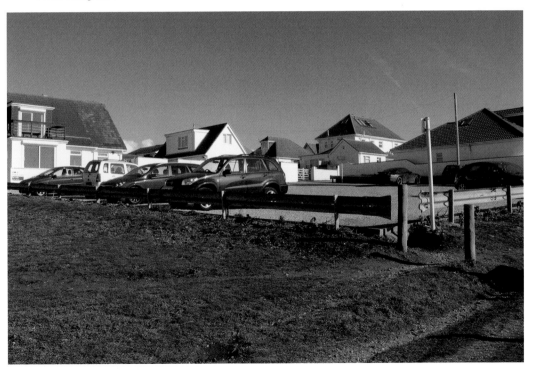

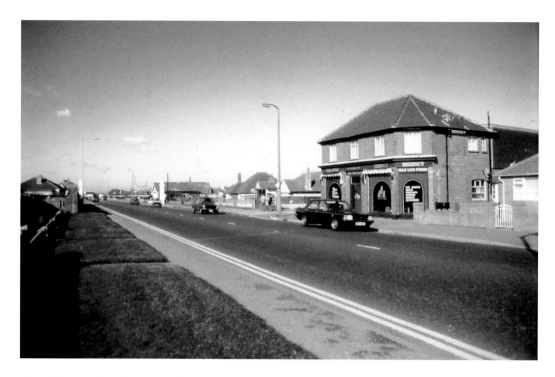

One of the very few businesses that is still going, the earlier photograph was taken in 1986 showing Regency Fireplaces, just the frontage has been modernised. The building is virtually the last one on the Coast Road before you reach Newhaven.

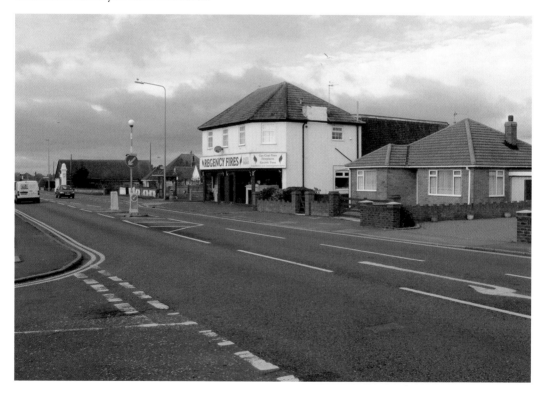

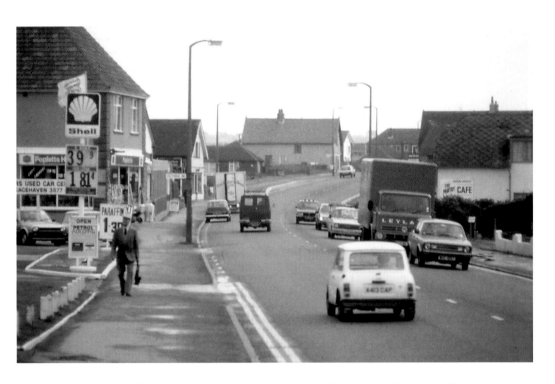

Petrol at the Shell Garage in 1986, was 39.9 p per litre or £1.84 per Gallon, the building behind was Popletts hardware and builders merchants. In early December 2008 petrol now unleaded, was just reduced to 91.9p per litre, the price at the time was volatile and was by Christmas 2008 only 86.9p Next door now is Haven Interiors and a large charity shop for Martlett's Hospice.

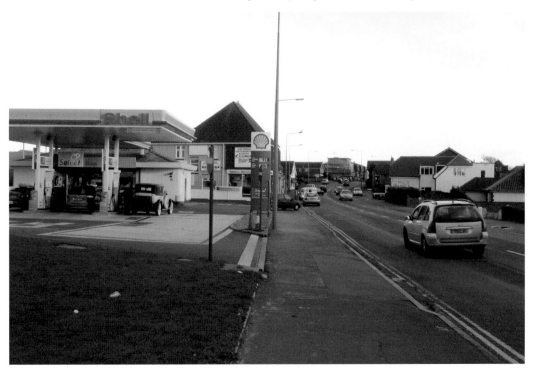

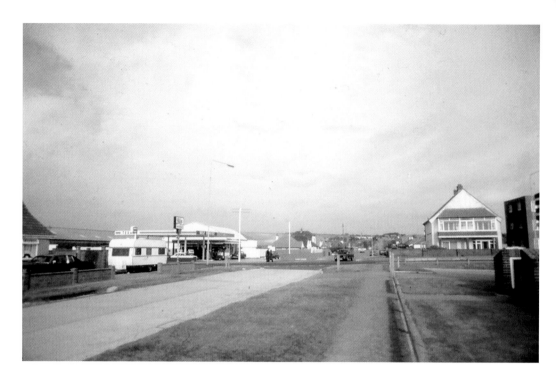

Bottom of Sussex Way in 1986 looking north to Telscombe Cliffs Way. The Texaco garage is still there and the restaurant to the left has changed hands but is still operating. Opposite the garage was a private house, today it is the home of a Motor Caravan Dealers.

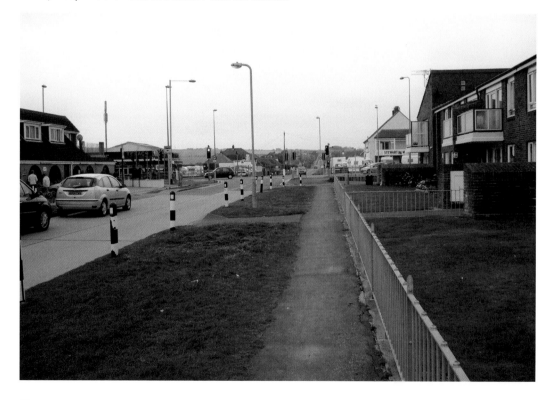

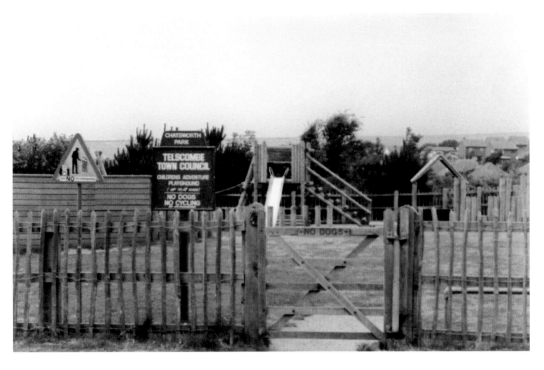

Chatsworth Park children's play area in 1986, is a bit more overgrown today but it is still popular with young children.

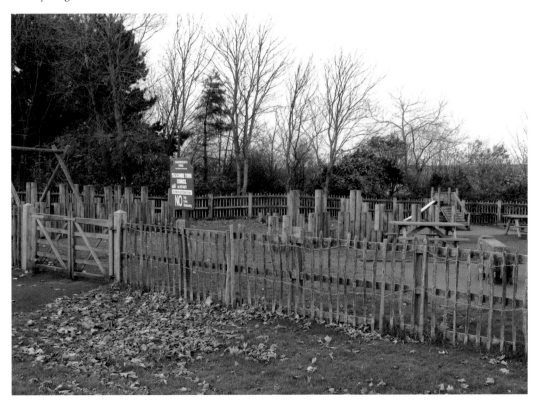

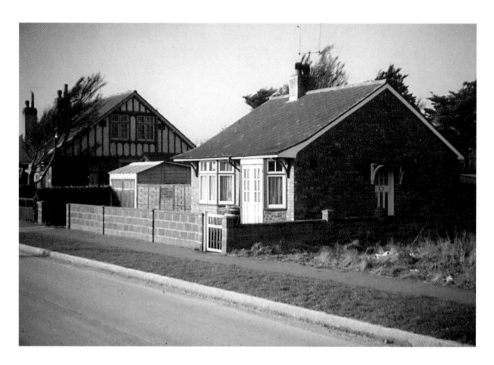

96 Arundel Road, was a single bungalow at the corner to Piddinghoe Avenue. At the time of the picture in 1967, just before it was sold, the view behind was of open fields. Today as a pair of semi-detached houses the view behind is of the new Bovis Homes estate, currently called Meridian End, construction of which only started in 2007.

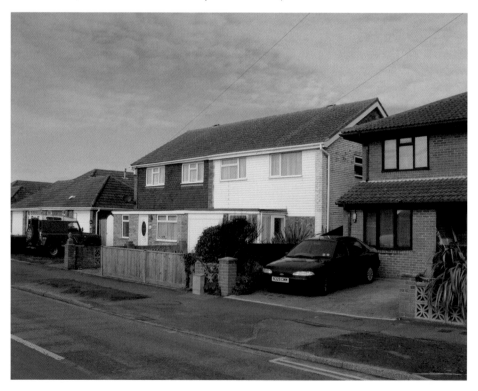

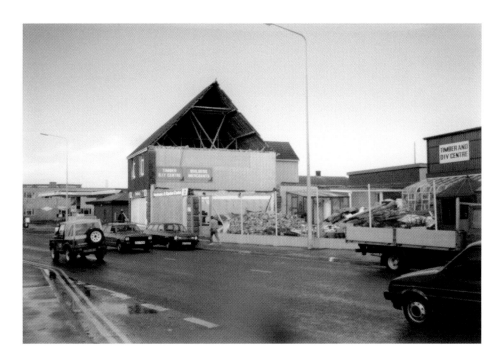

In October 1987 the south coast was hit by the Great Storm, and I took a couple of pictures. This was all that was left of Popletts DIY store and their garden centre, it virtually disappeared. Today it is the Martlett's Hospice shop.

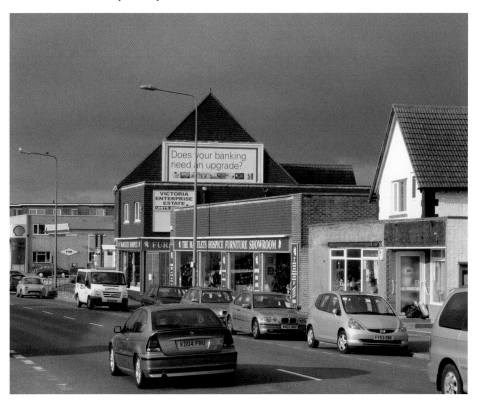

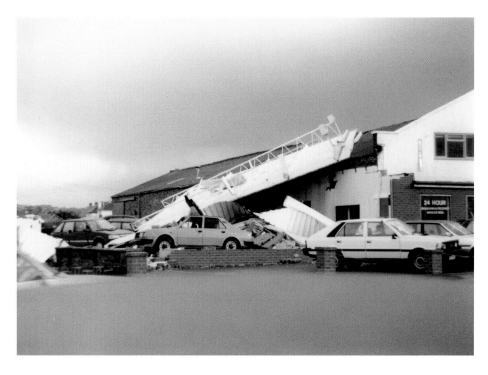

In Telscombe Cliffs Saltdean garage was a busy Skoda car dealership, in the October 1987 storm hardly a car survived. Now it is the home of the Bed Centre.

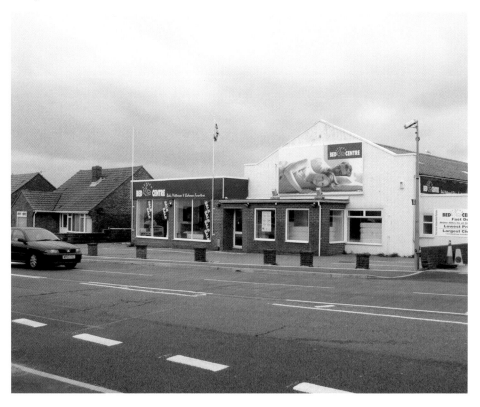

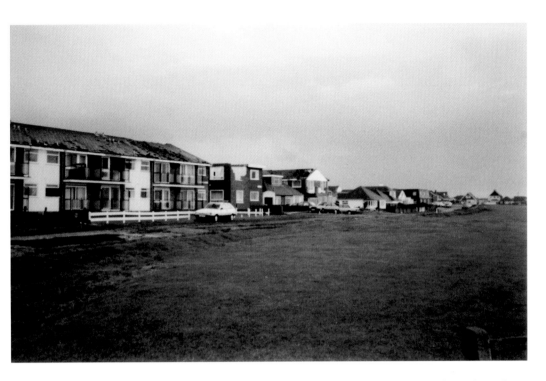

The Promenade suffered greatly in the October 1987 storm as can be seen hardly a flat or house has a roof. Fortunately homes can be repaired and you would not know anything ever happened.

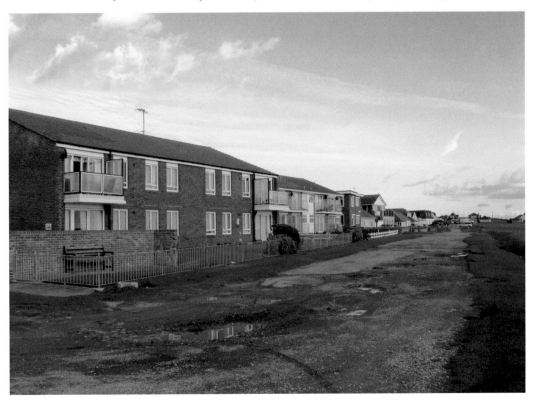

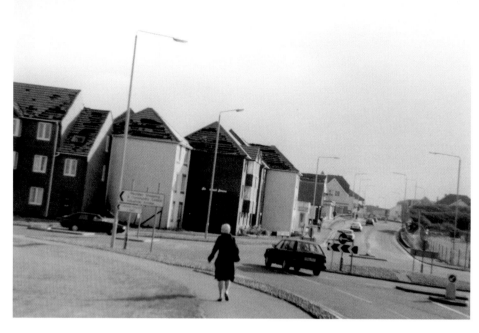

Homecoast House had only just been opened by McCarthy & Stone as sheltered retired housing when the storm struck in 1987. They lost many roof tiles, and today it looks as good as new.

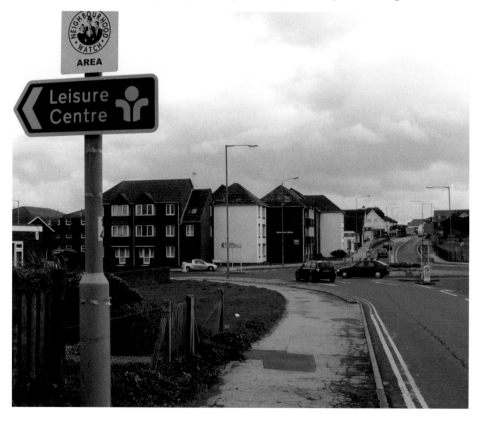

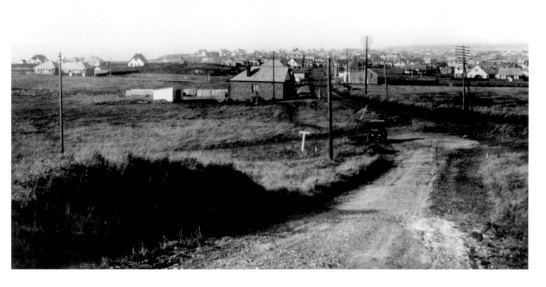

Finally a look back at what the town of Peacehaven would have looked like shortly after building started in 1920, taken from the highway. Now it can be seen as a thriving busy town situated on the very busy A259.

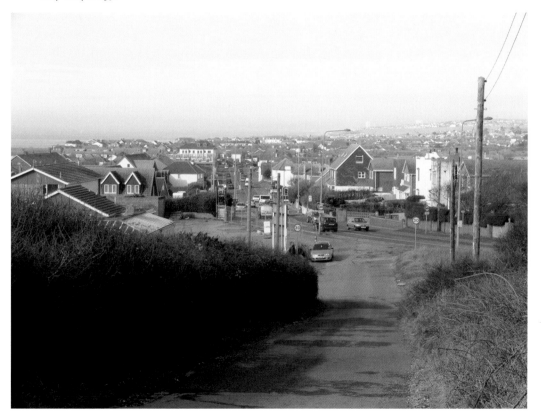

Acknowledgements

I would like to thank Brian Rutty, Adam Going and Ian Watson for pictures on pages 25, 35 and 85 respectively. Also those members of the former Peacehaven & Telscombe History Society who over the years let me take copies of their old pictures, a few of which are included here. Malcolm Troak and Valerie Mellor, for their invaluable help and knowledge, as fellow local historians. Much of the work would not have been possible without the help of the staff at National Archives, East Sussex, West Sussex and Kent County Record Offices, not forgetting those at the British Library's Newspaper Library. Finally a big thank you to my wife Shelley, for putting up with me during the writing of this book, and reviewing the first draft.

The Author

Born in Edgware, Middlesex, on his marriage moved to St Albans in Hertfordshire, before moving to Peacehaven with his wife and family in 1986. He continued his career in accountancy working mainly for solicitors. During the recession of the early 1990s he went to University as a mature student with the aim of finding a new career. Obtained his B.A. (honours) in Library and Information Studies at the University of Brighton in 1995, and completed his B.A. (open) with the Open University the following year. It was through study with the Open University that sparked his interest in history.

While a student Stanley had a part-time job at Peacehaven Town Council. It was while working there that he was asked to type the letter inviting people to a meeting to discuss the idea of forming a museum and history society. Since that inaugural meeting in 1995 he has remained secretary of the Peacehaven & Telscombe Historical Society, becoming chairman in 2004. Unfortunately the Society was wound up in 2008.

By 1999 firmly back working as a legal cashier, renewing his membership of the Institute of Legal Cashiers and Administrators. In 2001 he was elected to the Institute's Executive Committee.